Saint Peter's University Library
Withdrawn

Conflicting Conceptions

of

Curriculum

THE NATIONAL SOCIETY
FOR THE STUDY OF EDUCATION

Series on Contemporary Educational Issues
Kenneth J. Rehage, Series Editor

The 1974 Titles

Conflicting Conceptions of Curriculum, Elliot Eisner and Elizabeth
   Vallance, Editors
Crucial Issues in Testing, Ralph W. Tyler and Richard M. Wolf,
   Editors
Cultural Pluralism, Edgar G. Epps, Editor
Rethinking Educational Equality, Andrew Kopan and Herbert
   Walberg, Editors

The National Society for the Study of Education also publishes Year-
books which are distributed by the University of Chicago Press. Inquiries regarding all publications of the Society, as well as inquiries
about membership in the Society, may be addressed to the Secretary-
Treasurer, 5835 Kimbark Avenue, Chicago, 60637.

Committee on an Expanded Publication Program

Daniel U. Levine, Herbert Walberg, cochairmen

Edgar G. Epps   Raquel H. Montenegro
Robert J. Havighurst   William Spady
            Harriet Talmage
        Kenneth J. Rehage, ex officio

Board of Directors of the Society—1973

Jeanne Chall   John I. Goodlad
Luvern L. Cunningham   Robert J. Havighurst
N. L. Gage   Harold G. Shane

        Kenneth J. Rehage, ex officio
        Herman G. Richey, Editor

Conflicting Conceptions
of
Curriculum

Edited by

Elliot W. Eisner
and
Elizabeth Vallance

Stanford University

McCutchan Publishing Corporation
2526 Grove Street
Berkeley, California 94704

ISBN 8211-0411-X
Library of Congress Catalog Card Number 73-17616

© 1974 by McCutchan Publishing Corporation
Printed in the United States of America

B
570
E 425

Series Foreword

"Controversy in educational discourse," say the editors of this provocative collection of essays, "most often reflects a basic conflict in priorities concerning the form and content of curriculum and the goals toward which schools should strive. The intensity of the conflict and the apparent difficulty in resolving it can most often be traced to a failure to recognize these conflicting conceptions of curriculum."

The purpose of this volume is to assist those who engage in such discourse with the essential task of identifying and examining in a systematic way the assumptions underlying each of five common orientations toward the field of curriculum. As the editors point out, there are clearly alternate ways of formulating distinctive orientations to the field. The five formulations presented here, however, may well serve as a useful means of classifying views commonly taken in current arguments about curriculum.

Conflicting Conceptions of Curriculum is one of four titles in the 1974 Series on Contemporary Educational Issues published in paperback format under the auspices of the National Society for the Study of Education. Other titles in the Series are:

Crucial Issues in Testing, edited by Ralph W. Tyler and Richard M. Wolf;

v

Cultural Pluralism, edited by Edgar G. Epps;
Rethinking Educational Equality, edited by Andrew Kopan and Herbert Walberg.

With this new set of four volumes the Society continues its program, begun in 1971, of bringing out timely books that will provide a background for informed discussion of critical issues in education.

Kenneth J. Rehage
for the Committee on the Expanded
Publication Program of the
National Society for the Study
of Education

Contributors

Carl Bereiter, Professor of Applied Psychology, Ontario Institute for Studies in Education

Gary D. Brooks, Assistant Professor of Educational Administration and Director, Office of Institutional Studies, University of Texas

Richard W. Burns, Professor of Education, University of Texas, El Paso

Elliot W. Eisner, Professor of Education and Art, Stanford University

Robert Gagné, Professor of Educational Research, Florida State University

Ralph P. Goldman, Doctoral Candidate, Teachers College, Columbia University

P. H. Hirst, Professor of Education, University of Cambridge

Maurice P. Hunt, Professor of Educational Foundations, Fresno State College

Joseph S. Junell, College Supervisor, Central Washington State College, Ellensburg

John Mann, Assistant Professor of Education, Johns Hopkins University

Lawrence E. Metcalf, Professor of Secondary Education and Social Studies, University of Illinois

Harold J. Noah, Professor of Economics and Education, Teachers College, Columbia University

R. S. Peters, Professor of Education, Institute of Education, University of London

Philip H. Phenix, Professor of Philosophy and Education, Teachers College, Columbia University

Joseph J. Schwab, Visiting Fellow, Center for the Study of Democratic Institutions, Santa Barbara

Harold G. Shane, University Professor of Education, Indiana University

Robert E. Silverman, Chairman, Department of Psychology, University College of Arts and Science, New York University, Bronx

Elizabeth Vallance, Doctoral Candidate, School of Education, Stanford University

William H. Weber, Assistant Professor of Economics, Agnes Scott College

Contents

Introduction

Five Conceptions of Curriculum: Their Roots and Implications for Curriculum Planning

Elliot W. Eisner and *Elizabeth Vallance*

American education today, perhaps more than in the past, is studded with a variety of conflicting conceptions of the goals, content, and organization of curriculum. The complexity of educational thought is manifested not only in the diversity of papers presented in professional meetings and printed in professional journals; it is also apparent in debates, discussions, and controversies dramatizing school board and PTA meetings, and it is reflected and amplified by the involvement of the general public through the mass media.

The controversies we refer to deal on an overt level with issues surrounding alternative schools, conflicting roles of vocational and academic education in the school curriculum, concern with a student's academic achievement in the "solid" subjects, educational admonitions to enable children to "learn how to learn," purposes and uses of accountability procedures, and the use of input-output models of educational practice. On a more fundamental level, however, the debates and conflicts generated by each of these themes derive necessarily from the degree of incompatibility between the values and goals underlying each side of the issue being debated. Controversy in educational discourse most often reflects a basic conflict in priorities concerning the form and content of curriculum and the goals toward which schools should strive; the intensity of the conflict and the apparent difficulty in resolving it can most often be traced to a failure to recognize conflicting conceptions of curriculum. Public educational discourse frequently does not bother to examine its conceptual underpinnings.

To the student of curriculum, then, the richness of issues and values in the field provides an arena that can be either a dynamic and stimulating resource or a conceptual jungle difficult to define and almost impossible to manage. Students of education—both those preparing for practical work in curriculum and instruction and those already in the field—might find helpful a set of signposts that distinguishes between conflicting orientations. Those in school administration, particularly those who in some ways link the school and the community, might be better able to help their staff and the community understand the issues at hand if they themselves could distinguish between the conceptual orientations of the different alternatives presented to them.

This book has been prepared to help identify the orientations that emerge from diverse alternative prescriptions for the content, goals, and organization of the curriculum. We have tried especially to enable both professional educators and lay people to recognize and evaluate these orientations in terms of the goals and assumptions embedded within them; the articles reprinted here were selected to exemplify what we consider to be the major orientations to curriculum that currently prevail in the literature.

The development of a set of distinctions concerning the content of published articles about curriculum is somewhat arbitrary. The five general orientations that we have identified do not necessarily exhaust the ways in which positions can be characterized or identified, and there is nothing sacred about the labels or distinctions we offer. They can constitute a powerful tool for analyzing the implications of an otherwise confusing body of arguments, however. The orientations refer to a range of distinct conceptual biases that emerged repeatedly in a rather comprehensive survey of current literature in and related to the field. The orientations, while not exhaustive, are comprehensive in that they identify a broad range of very different approaches to questions persistently asked in the curriculum field: What can and should be taught to whom, when, and how? The way these questions are answered is influenced largely by the assumptions through which they are approached in the first place. These assumptions, and the regularity with which they emerge as distinguishable patterns, define the five orientations that have been formulated: the cognitive processes approach, curriculum as technology, curriculum for self-actualization and consummatory experiences, curriculum for social reconstruction, and academic rationalism.

The answers to the major questions in curriculum—and indeed the questions themselves—are most often couched in terms of the assumptions embedded in each orientation. Before outlining the five orientations, there is a brief indication of some of the considerations that went into developing them.

Some Viewpoints Not Treated Directly

Some important criteria may seem to have been neglected in defining the five orientations to curricular thought offered below, but there were reasons for their exclusion. The first orientation to compete for inclusion in the scheme is that continuum implied by the "child-centered versus society-centered" distinction. The child-centered orientation can be traced back to the ideas of Quintillian, Comenius, Rousseau, and Pestalozzi, while the society-centered orientation emanates from the ideas of Aristotle, Calvin, and Jefferson. In more recent times John Dewey and the progressives gave new life to the distinction, and it has emerged full blown today with controversies over free schools, open classrooms, and other humanist-oriented innovations in schooling. The assumptions underlying the child-centered versus the society-centered distinction are crucial for understanding educational thought today and can illuminate some of the problems in evaluating both the post-Sputnik push for the "solid" subjects and the current movement in alternative education. The continuum is implicit in some of the distinctions we have drawn. If we do not deal explicitly with this dimension, however, it is largely because the distinction does not seem to contribute further insight into the complexity of current thought in curriculum. Significant educational dialogue today does not speak as clearly in these terms as it once did; the issues have shifted and become more refined; the child-society distinction today has lost the crystalline character it enjoyed in the past.

It might also be defensible to organize educational writings along a spectrum that has values education, on one end, and skills training, on the other, or moral education as opposed to the three R's. This, too, is a salient distinction in education. It reflects the difference between seeing schools as an agent for moral uplift and seeing the school as a purely functional means of providing the survival skills necessary for the maintenance of civilization. This criterion would emphasize the difference between a broadly optimistic vision of what the schools can be expected to do and the narrower interpretation of their capacities; we see it in the difference between Aristotle's or Jefferson's faith in education as the moral backbone of a democracy and Calvin's more immediate demand that schools teach the children to read the Bible. More recently, the difference is reflected in the argument of Kohlberg[1] that the schools actively intervene in the development of moral judgment and that of Bereiter[2] and others whose concern is almost entirely with the transmission of basic skills. The former argument is value laden and urges an ethical commitment; the latter argument claims to be functional and virtually value neutral. While this distinction is useful in evaluating curriculum proposals, we refer to the value-skills dimension only secondarily since curricular dialogue is seldom presented specifically in these terms. The distinction is implicit in some of the differences among the five orientations, such as that between social reconstructionism, on the one hand, and the cognitive processes approach, on the other.

Psychological models also differentiate between conceptualizations of schooling. Such differences can often be reduced to a disagreement as to the model of learning presumed by each since any conceptualization of education reflects some assumptions as to how children learn—ranging from behavioral S-R models at one extreme to humanist or existential models at the other. But to specify a psychological continuum would be hazardous since psychology itself is at least as multidimensional as education and, furthermore, it is difficult to obtain agreement on the terminology. For these reasons we have chosen not to differentiate explicitly the writings in curriculum by the psychological models to which they implicitly refer. Nevertheless, it is clear that any comprehensive scheme of curriculum issues must be able at least to accommodate these differences; the orientations we have formulated seem to make such accommodation possible.

The present-future dimension is another reasonable criterion for differentiating curriculum thought. It is possible to distinguish a set of curriculum orientations according to whether they refer to curriculum as a present "lived in" experience, as an end, or whether they see curriculum as an instrument toward some future goal, as a means. This dimension is a rich one; it refers partially to the distinction between child-centered and society-centered education and can be linked conceptually to certain psychological models as well. The present-future distinction also suggests some criteria for viewing a curriculum proposal as adaptive (fitting the child to deal with here and now), or as reconstructive (providing the tools for dealing with and shaping the future). It is deliberately implied in some of the distinctions we draw in the selection of articles. We have not used the present-future dimension as a major criterion for structuring these readings, however, largely because the central issues in educational discussion do not revolve around the time orientation itself. Though it is a useful descriptive device, it is not a fully salient criterion. The five orientations presented in this short book, then, refer only secondarily to these distinctions, though they should be flexible enough to accommodate them.

It is important to note that, in addition to the above distinctions, there are a number of what might more properly be called pertinent educational issues or sensitive areas susceptible to curriculum policy decisions to which the scheme does not directly refer. These issues include the debates over religious education, cultural pluralism, community control of curriculum, and the "hidden curriculum" of the school. Although these issues must be acknowledged as relevant aspects of the curriculum field, they are essentially points of contention which must themselves ultimately be referred to the conceptualizations of schooling underlying them. The reader may wish to work with them on his own; one test of the scheme presented here may be to determine whether such issues can be profitably evaluated in terms of the scheme.

Five Orientations to Curriculum

The development of cognitive processes. This approach to curriculum is primarily concerned with the refinement of intellectual operations. It refers only rarely to curriculum content, focusing, instead, on the how rather than the what of education. Aiming to develop a sort of technology of the mind, it sees the central problem of curriculum as that of sharpening the intellectual processes and developing a set of cognitive skills that can be applied to learning virtually anything.

This approach is process oriented in two senses: it identifies the goals of schooling as providing a repertoire of essentially content-independent cognitive skills applicable to a variety of situations, and it is concerned with understanding the processes by which learning occurs in the classroom. The interactive relationship between the learner and the material is of prime concern; "education" refers to the dynamics of learning, and, as such, this conceptualization of schooling is necessarily open-ended and growth oriented. Since it does not deal with specific content and therefore makes no reference to any content "givens" in educational goals, the cognitive processes approach sees the learner as an interactive and adaptive element in a system which, if given the correct intellectual tools, could grow almost indefinitely. The problem of the educator and curriculum specialist, then, is to identify the most salient and efficient intellectual processes through which learning occurs and to provide the setting and structure for their development. Education is seen as an impartial enabling mechanism; specific intellectual skills are secured as tools for adapting to and shaping future situations.

This orientation to curriculum focuses on the child and refers to the learning process per se rather than to the broader social context in which it occurs. It aims to provide the student with a sort of intellectual autonomy that will enable him to make his own selections and interpretations of the situations encountered beyond the context of schooling. Though educational writers embracing the cognitive processes approach may acknowledge that schooling has effects beyond intellectual development, they assert that the proper concern of curriculum is still the development of cognitive skills, skills that presumably transfer to a wide variety of situations outside of schools. An article by Carl Bereiter illustrates this latter position: "Schools do not and cannot successfully educate—that is, influence how children turn out in any important way. The most they can do successfully is provide child care and training"—where "training" means producing "a certain kind of performance in the child. What the child does with his required skill, how it is integrated into his personality, is a concern that lies beyond training."[3]

The cognitive processes approach is a particularly salient orientation in curriculum thinking today, and it seems to grow more potent as psychologists develop greater confidence in their ability to identify the mechanisms through which thinking develops. Historically, this approach is related to the nineteenth-century tradition of faculty psychology, which held that the key to learning lay in developing the muscles of the mind as it were, and it assumed that strengthening the various mental "faculties" would enable the individual to apply these cognitive abilities to learning any sort of content. This concern with building generalizable intellectual skills has been greatly elaborated in recent years and is now most fully expounded in the developmental psychology of Jerome Bruner[4] and that of Robert Gagné.[5] The cognitive processes approach has stimulated the development of curricula such as the "science curriculum" of the American Association for the Advancement of Science, which was organized around the development of specific cognitive processes. This approach illustrates the way in which assumptions about how children learn influence the development of educational programs.

Curriculum as technology. This approach to schooling, like the cognitive processes approach, focuses on process. It is also concerned with the how rather than the what of education. It conceptualizes the function of curriculum as essentially one of finding efficient means to a set of predefined, nonproblematic ends. As a process approach, curriculum technology differs from cognitive processes in its focus of attention. It is concerned not with the processes of knowing or learning, but with the technology by which knowledge is communicated and "learning" is facilitated. Making little or no reference to content, it is concerned with developing a technology of instruction. The focus is less on the learner or even on his relationship to the material than on the more practical problem of efficiently packaging and presenting the material to him. A step removed both from the individuality of the learner and from the content which defines the curricular experience, the technologists claim to be developing a value-free system.

The language of the curriculum technologist is as efficient as the system it hopes to produce. It is concise, even terse, often skeletally logical, crystalline, and to the point. Articles reflecting this orientation are very frequently only a page or two long. (The reader is referred to *Educational Technology* for the fullest exposure to this mode of thought, though it appears elsewhere, also.) The curriculum technology approach speaks the language of production; curriculum technologists see curriculum as an input to supply and demand systems. They talk in terms of industrial systems, accountability, or systems analysis. Their vocabulary is one of input, output, entry behavior, cybernetic models, biofeedback mechanisms, stimulus and reinforcement, and systems to "produce" learning. Theirs is a self-confident language. Although curriculum technologists do not claim to have all the answers, they ask questions in terms that imply that answers do exist somewhere and need only to be discovered. Curriculum is viewed as a technological process, as a means to producing whatever ends an industrial model education system might generate. As Silverman states (also see Chapter 4),

the problems associated with teaching are interwoven with questions about the retention and transfer of learning. Any model which purports to deal with learning must, if it is to prove useful, deal also with the conditions that effect retention and transfer. In terms of the S-R reinforcement model, questions about retention become questions about the conditions that control and maintain responses.[6]

The curriculum-technology approach rests on certain "stable" assumptions about the nature of learning, namely that learning does occur in certain systematic and predictable ways and that it can be made more efficient if only a powerful method for controlling it can be perfected. The learner is seen neither as problematic nor as a particularly dynamic element in the system; the real task of the educator arises in organizing the material sometime before the learner ever enters the classroom.

Because it does assume certain constants in the learner's role, however, this approach cannot be as value-neutral as the exuberant language of the articles included here would indicate; indeed, it can be argued that this orientation is highly value saturated since any commitment to method has inevitable consequences for the goals and content of the education it would serve. The failure to articulate these implications is perhaps as strong a value statement as any content bias might be, for to adopt the language of technology without acknowledging the other value systems that have traditionally dominated education, and that might therefore be in conflict with it, is too easily to discredit the possibility of alternatives. While this cautionary criterion applies to any conceptualization of schooling which believes so robustly in the validity of its own convictions, it is particularly relevant to the sudden self-confidence of educational technology. The three articles we have included in this volume offer an introduction to the issues raised by this conceptualization of curriculum.

Self-actualization, or curriculum as consummatory experience. Strongly and deliberately value saturated, this approach refers to personal purpose and to the need for personal integration, and it views the function of the curriculum as providing personally satisfying consummatory experiences for each individual learner. It is child centered, autonomy and growth oriented, and education is seen as an enabling process that would provide the means to personal liberation and development.

This approach focuses sharply on content. Unlike the cognitive process or curriculum technology approaches, the concern is very much for what is taught in school. It conceptualizes education as a liberating force, a means of helping the individual discover things for himself. Schooling is seen as a vital and potentially enriching experience in its own right, and content as present experience is a major focus of concern. Interestingly, this orientation is concerned almost as much with process as the two preceding orientations, but in a different sense. Rather than directing itself to how the curriculum should be organized, it formulates the goals of education in dynamic personal process terms. It emphasizes personal growth and, therefore, though it sees the curriculum as a consummatory experience in itself, it is also necessarily somewhat reformist. It implies a need to break bonds, to change, for the development of personal integrity and autonomy is seen as problematic in the face of broader social pressures to the contrary. It is reconstructionist in a very personalized sense.

Unlike the more strictly process-oriented approaches considered so far, the self-actualizers assign education a much grander task. They demand that schooling, through the curriculum, enter fully into the child's life. They assume that it can do so, their criticism being that it has always done so, but without acknowledging the responsibilities involved. They see education as a necessarily pervasive influence that has been handled inadequately and very stultifyingly. They demand that the curriculum become better orchestrated to fulfill its potential as a liberating process by providing integrated experience. As content, then, the curriculum is seen as an end in itself. As a stage in the life process, education would provide both content and tools for further self-discovery.

The language of this group of writers is rich and elaborate, dealing in levels of subtlety apparently unimagined by technologists of either variety; it is broadly integrative, a language interwoven with the language of humanism, of existentialism, and of existential psychology. Phenix represents this view very clearly (also see Chapter 6):

A curriculum of transcendence provides the context of engendering, gestating, expecting, and celebrating the moments of singular awareness and inner illumination when each person comes into the consciousness of his inimitable personal being. It is not characterized so much by the objective content of study as by the atmosphere created by those who comprise the learning community. Its opposite is the engineering outlook that regards the learner as material to be formed by means of a variety of technical procedures.[7]

The self-actualizers share a passionate orientation to education. We have included two articles, one by Philip Phenix, quoted above, and another by Joseph Junell[8] that questions the traditional, rationally oriented basis of education. The reader is referred also to the excellent work by Maxine Greene,[9] to Abraham Maslow's[10] work relating humanistic psychology to educational programs, and to the work by Fred Newmann and Donald Oliver[11] and that by Kenneth Benne[12] on the role of education in creating community. All of these writers conceive of education as an integrative, synthesizing force, as a total experience responsible to the individual's needs for growth and personal integrity.

Social reconstruction-relevance. With this orientation there is a strong emphasis on the role of education and curriculum content within the larger social context. Social reconstructionists typically stress societal needs over individual needs; the overall goals of education are dealt with in terms of total experience, rather than using the immediate processes which they imply. Social reform and responsibility to the future of society are primary.

The social reconstructionist orientation to curriculum is hardly new. The refrain runs through much of the history of educational reform, and it is a characteristic of Western society that schools, more than any other institution, are called upon to serve as an agent for social change. The social view of schooling examines education and curriculum in terms of their relation to the social issues of the day. An approach in which social values, and often political positions, are clearly stated, social reconstructionism demands that schools recognize and respond to their role as a bridge between what is and what might be, between the real and the ideal. It is the traditional view of schooling as the bootstrap by which society can change itself. Within this approach to curriculum, there are two distinct branches; it embraces both a present and a future orientation, both an adaptive and a reformist interpretation of social relevance. The psychological model underlying both versions is a social-psychological one that views individual development and the quality of the social context as interdependent. Both branches of the social reconstruction approach seek to develop a better "fit" between the individual and society. The first and basically adaptive approach views social issues and change as a crucial context for personal development. It foresees enormous changes in society and asks that curriculum provide the tools for individual survival in an unstable and changing world. This survival-oriented bias to the relevance issue defines relevance in personal terms, advocating a curriculum that would make the individual better able to keep up and function effectively in a rapidly changing world. This "adaptive" group includes educational technologists who would change curriculum to correspond more closely to technological changes in information processing, and data collection; reformists, such as those of the Parkway School in Philadelphia, who seek to have the curriculum reflect current "real-life" situations; and writers like John Mann (see Chapter 8), who demand that current issues of political power be incorporated into the curriculum so that students can learn to deal with them more effectively and creatively as such issues emerge. Mann writes: "What I envision . . . is a movement to design a progressive curriculum specifically for these angry, radical students, in which the study of educational policy formation and of the policies of schools would converge in and be reinforced, corrected, refined and deepened in the practical experience of actually formulating educational policy and struggling to enact it."[13]

The reformist wing of the relevance orientation is more vigorous and demands more of schools. This truly reconstructionist view demands that individuals be better equipped to deal with change but also that they be educated to intervene actively to shape the changes. While all sides of the social reconstruction-relevance orientation view curriculum as the means by which students learn to deal with social issues, the adaptive group is more conservative, asking for survival instruments; the reformists are more aggressively leadership conscious. This reconstructionist group includes, then, those who advocate adaptation as one means of effecting smooth change and the more aggressively idealistic writers that are found in the "futures" research groups, in "peace education" coalitions and in recent works by people like Michael Scriven[14] and Ivan Illich.[15]

Academic rationalism. The most tradition-bound of the five orientations, academic rationalism is primarily concerned with enabling the young to acquire the tools to participate in the Western cultural tradition and with providing access to the greatest ideas and objects that man has created. Those embracing this orientation tend to hold that since schools cannot try to teach everything or even everything deemed worth knowing, their legitimate function is that of cultural transmission in the most specific sense: to cultivate the child's intellect by providing him with opportunities to acquire the most powerful products of man's intelligence. These products are found, for the most part, in the established disciplines. To become educated means to be able to read and understand those works that the great disciplines have produced, a heritage that is at least as old as the beginnings of Greek civilization. The curriculum, it is argued, should emphasize the classic disciplines through which man inquires since these disciplines, almost by definition, provide concepts and criteria through which thought acquires precision, generality, and power; such disciplines exemplify intellectual activity at its best. To construct a curriculum that includes "practical" learning such as driver training, homemaking, and vocational education dilutes the quality of education and robs students of the opportunity to study those subjects that reflect man's enduring quest for meaning. The wise schoolmaster knows that not all subject matters are created equal, and he selects the content of his educational program with this principle in mind.

Robert Maynard Hutchins has long advocated this approach, and he offered a classic statement of academic rationalism in 1953:

Liberal education consists of training in the liberal arts and of understanding the leading ideas that have animated mankind . . . the great productions of the human mind are the common heritage of all mankind. They supply the framework through which we understand one another and without which all factual data and area studies and exchange of persons among countries are trivial and futile. They are the voices in the Great Conversation that constitutes the civilization of the dialogue.

Now, if ever, we need an education that is designed to bring out our common humanity rather than to indulge our individuality.[16]

The foregoing characterization has, however, undergone a significant evolution in recent years. A glance at any high school curriculum will reveal that "the disciplines" still hold strong sway; what has changed is the nature of the argument by which they are defended. Emerging in the curriculum literature currently is a strong orientation toward "the structure of knowledge"—a significant rethinking of the traditional disciplines in an effort to determine what it is about their respective content that distinguishes them from each other. This new questioning of the disciplines still assumes the validity of the subject matter divisions, but, rather than merely identifying them, it asks why the divisions have held up for so long. Writers such as Joseph Schwab[17] and Robert Bridgham[18] are beginning to rephrase the traditional academic rationalist approach by examining the logical and structural bases for the division. The healthy spirit of inquiry evidenced by their writings suggests that the traditional "disciplines" approach is questionable. More significantly, however, the current controversy is adding a new dimension to this orientation. By digging to find the structural bases of the disciplines, the structure of knowledge question is bringing a new and sophisticated concern with process into a traditionally content-saturated conceptualization of education. Dewey suggested long ago that the "logical" and "psychological" structure of content might be two different things. Academic rationalism survived for centuries without recognizing this crucial distinction, but recent work in refining subject matter curricula along structural lines, such as the School Mathematics Study Group materials, indicates that this most traditional orientation to education is undergoing substantial change.

Academic rationalism is alive and well. The problem is to understand why we are so defensive about it, and many participants in educational enterprises are. The structure of knowledge orientation is a dynamic new development within a very old field. A recognition of the sources and implications of this orientation is essential in any educational dialogue that claims to understand the boundaries of the curriculum field.

A Cautionary Word Concerning Three Curriculum Fallacies

As we review the literature concerning curriculum, it has become apparent that three fallacies frequently emerge from curricular arguments: formalism, content, and universalism.

The fallacy of formalism encourages the belief that what is really important in educational programs is how children learn, not what they learn. Those committing this fallacy frequently point out that knowledge is changing at an exceedingly rapid rate—it has doubled within the past decade, although it is never made clear how this "doubling" is measured—and that the major goal of the school should be to help children "learn how to learn."

The demand that children be taught how to learn has an attractive humanist ring. When schools are being criticized for being stiff and bookish and when the student's role is seen as simply regurgitating facts and conclusions, any criticism of formalism assumes the character of an antidote to a moribund educational practice and conveys a dynamic image centered on inquiry and self-initiated learning. Educational technologists, both hard-core "curricular technologists" and "technology of the mind" (cognitive processes) educators are particularly susceptible to this fallacy. Recognition of it as a fallacy should limit the validity of any technology or process-oriented conceptualization of schooling.

Any form of learning, including inquiry and self-initiated learning, can deal with the intellectually trivial as well as with the intellectually significant. To argue that the form of education is the most important aspect of schooling is to disregard the very concepts and criteria that make inquiry possible in the first place. Indeed, it was lack of attention to the "progressive organization of subject matter" that so concerned John Dewey when he reviewed the practices of those involved in "Progressive Education." Yet today's critics of American schools are frequently so critical of the formal aspect of educational practice in their zeal to change an outdated structure that they neglect the very intellectual resources necessary for understanding.

The fallacy of content, as might be expected, complements the formalist fallacy. Those who commit this fallacy are preoccupied with the importance of what rather than with how students study. They overemphasize "solid" content, content that is believed to be intellectually rigorous and difficult and that, by its very nature, is presumed to make the necessary strenuous intellectual demands upon students. Of the five orientations we have identified, academic rationalists are perhaps most susceptible to this fallacy. It frequently is seen in the admonitions of the Council for Basic Education whose members, like others concerned with achieving quality in American education, frequently decry what they see as a trivialization of curriculum in an attempt to placate student demands for relevance. They claim that educators have, in the name of meeting individual needs, withheld the vast intellectual tradition that is every person's legacy from the past.

Like the fallacy of formalism, the fallacy of content has attractive features. All ideas are not created equal, and some concepts and generalizations, some ideas and products of past inquiry are more useful and more profound than others. To deny students access to the very best intellectual and aesthetic products that civilization has created is to deny them the core of what education can provide. But the products of science and of art do not speak of themselves. Ideas become instrumental and works of art become aesthetic only when they are approached through appropriate modes of inquiry and perception. (In the sciences, for example, conclusions have no cognitive status independent of the theory, method, and criteria against which they are developed and tested). Understanding science and appreciating the arts requires active engagement on the student's part, and emphasizing content to the exclusion of those modes of inquiry that produced it is to misconceive the nature of content itself. Furthermore, the disposition to become a creator as well as a consumer of intellectual and artistic products, a disposition that schools should try to foster, is frequently hampered by those who perpetuate the content fallacy. To avoid this fallacy requires attention to the form as well as the content of education. Both how and what students learn in school are of fundamental educational significance, and failure to appreciate their reciprocity has led many to subscribe to the fallacies of formalism and of content.

The third fallacy appearing in the literature on curriculum is an extension of the fallacy of content. It is the fallacy of universalism, which rests on the belief that some fundamental content areas or

topics are of universal significance regardless of the particular characteristics of the student whom the school is intended to serve. This
fallacy leads to a perpetual hunt for the "best" curriculum as though
there were one program that would be best for everyone of a particular age, regardless of other characteristics. Insofar as social reconstructionists attempt to establish global social reform values to the
exclusion of considering individual differences of ability or context,
this fallacy might define the useful limits of such an orientation.
Academic rationalists often tend to commit the fallacy of universalism in their quest for an educational program suitable to all.

An even more important effect of this fallacy, however, is that it
removes curriculum decision making from the arena of the empirical
study of its context, placing it, instead, in the arena of rhetoric. The
task of an advocate of a particular educational view becomes that of
persuading others to accept it rather than to treat it as an opportunity to inquire into conditions necessary for adequate curriculum decision making. If the new math or science is good, so the fallacy holds,
then surely it is good for everybody.

The fallacy of universalism is essentially conservative. Once the
sacrosanct subject matters have been defined, further change is resisted. Tradition and the status quo usually are accepted. This fallacy
is operating when we note how seldom discussions about the content
of the curriculum produce suggestions of an iconoclastic nature.
Most curricular recommendations accept the present array of content
as given and focus on rearranging or supplementing, rather than replacing, what already exists.

In Conclusion

These five curriculum orientations and three fallacies that can be
associated with curriculum have been identified to help clarify the
angles from which curriculum theorists, educators outside the curriculum field, and lay people approach decisions about curriculum.
Like any general scheme or set of distinctions, this approach has
assets and liabilities. The categories do, however, simplify and organize a complex field and in that sense they can economize thought
and function as a kind of mnemonic device that can be used to mine
an extremely rich vein in education. Again, like any general scheme,
the simplified version is never as detailed or as rich as the particular

area where specific decisions need to be made. In that sense, it over-simplifies. We have not determined, for example, how consistently any given orientation tends to be held even by its strongest advocate, or how its applicability varies depending upon the age level of the students to be served by a program. Nor do we know how much orientations are compromised, negotiated, and combined in the actual decision-making process. We do not know the relationships between orientations that dominate at school board meetings and those that dominate in particular classrooms within a school district. And, what is more significant, we know even less about the relationship between orientations reflected in professional journals, from which the five orientations were distilled, and how they actually function in either the school board meeting or the classroom situation.

Despite these limitations, which hold for any general classification as well as for theory, the schema we have formulated enables those interested in curriculum to make distinctions that are more useful than those generated by philosophic categories such as pragmatism, realism, and idealism, and it is more refined than any suggested by student-centered, subject-centered, or society-centered approaches to curriculum. The five curriculum orientations exemplified in the articles that follow are part of a larger intellectual tradition than that of the curriculum field itself. Each approach or orientation is manifested in other fields bearing upon education: for example, the cognitive process orientation has its roots in faculty psychology; the technological orientation grows out of time-and-motion study; academic rationalism is related to rational humanism. The model provides another way of revealing the ramifications of intellectual developments in fields that at first glance seemed removed from education. The ideas propounded by any given curricular argument can usually be traced to an established, well-articulated tradition of normative inquiry. It is imperative that educators recognize the larger philosophical differences that their conflicts so systematically reflect. It would seem that a sensitivity to intellectual history, particularly as this history reflects changing conceptualizations of the possibilities and limitations of learning, is an essential ingredient in curriculum analyses.

This work makes no attempt to provide answers to questions about what schools should teach or how any curriculum should be organized. In a sense, the volume is analytical and technical. It presents a schema, it explains why it was chosen, and it provides exemplary articles for each of the categories. We hope that readers will find these categories useful for organizing their thoughts concerning the goals, content, and organization of any curriculum.

Notes

1. Lawrence Kohlberg, "Moral Education in the School: A Developmental Vice," *School Review* 74 (Spring 1966), 1-30.

2. Carl Bereiter, "Schools without Education," *Harvard Educational Review* 42 (August 1972), 390-413.

3. *Ibid.*, 391-92.

4. Jerome Bruner, *The Process of Education* (Cambridge: Harvard University Press, 1960).

5. Robert M. Gagné, "Educational Technology as Technique," *Educational Technology* 8 (November 1968), 5-13.

6. Robert E. Silverman, "Using the S-R Reinforcement Model," *Ibid.* (March 1968), 10-11.

7. Philip H. Phenix, "Transcendence and the Curriculum," *Teachers College Record* 73 (December 1971), 279.

8. J. S. Junell, "Is Rational Man Our First Priority?" *Phi Delta Kappan* 52 (November 1970), 147-53.

9. Maxine Greene, "The Arts in a Global Village," *Educational Leadership* 26 (Fall 1969), 439-46, and "Curriculum and Consciousness," *Teachers College Record* 73 (December 1971), 253-69.

10. Abraham H. Maslow, "Some Educational Implications of the Humanistic Psychologies," *Harvard Educational Review* 38 (Fall 1968) 685-96.

11. F. M. Newmann and D. W. Oliver, "Education and Community," *Ibid.*, 37 (Winter 1967), 61-106.

12. Kenneth Benne, *Education in the Quest for Identity and Community* (Columbus: College of Education, Ohio State University, 1962).

13. John S. Mann, "Political Power and the High School Curriculum," *Educational Leadership* 28 (October 1970), 25-26.

14. Michael Scriven, "Education for Survival," in K. Ryan and J. Cooper (eds.), *Kaleidoscope* (Boston: Houghton-Mifflin, 1972), 272-99.

15. Ivan Illich, *De-Schooling Society* (New York: Harper & Row, 1971).

16. Robert M. Hutchins, *The Conflict in Education in a Democratic Society* (New York: Harper & Brothers, 1953), 83, 89-90.

17. Joseph J. Schwab, "Structure of the Disciplines: Meanings and Significances," in G. W. Ford and L. Pugno (eds.), *The Structure of Knowledge and the Curriculum* (Chicago: Rand-McNally, 1964), 6-30.

18. Robert G. Bridgham, "Conceptions of Science and the Learning of Science," *School Review* 78 (November 1969), 25-40.

Part One
Curriculum as the Development
of Cognitive Processes

The cognitive process orientation to curriculum seeks to develop a repertoire of cognitive skills that are applicable to a wide range of intellectual problems. In this view subject matter, as typically defined, is considered instrumental to the development of intellectual abilities that can be used in areas other than those in which the processes were originally refined. For example, content in history or in biology is considered less important than the development of the student's ability to infer, to speculate, to deduce, or to analyze. These abilities, it is argued, will endure long after the particular content or knowledge is forgotten or rendered obsolete by new knowledge.

The two chapters in this section illustrate the cognitive processes approach in different ways. Carl Bereiter, in his analysis of schooling in Chapter 1, attempts to identify those aspects of development which schooling is capable of furthering. He argues that the greatest strength of schooling is in the development of cognitive skills. Bereiter's conception of curriculum would focus on this area and would discount other, less realistic claims as to what schooling can accomplish. Richard Burns and Gary Brooks, in Chapter 2, detail some of the kinds of goals permitted by Bereiter's formulation, criticizing the educational system for its emphasis on static, factual knowledge and arguing that curriculum should assume responsibility for the development of concept-formation skills, processing behaviors, and problem-solving abilities.

1. Elementary School: Necessity or Convenience?

Carl Bereiter

Ivan Illich[1] has thought deeply about what people need in order to learn. He has concluded that they do not need schools. They need, says Illich, access to things—not only to specifically educational things like books, but also to the practical things of their world. Then they need access to models, to people who practice the skills or behaviors they wish to learn. They need access to peers who share their interests and with whom they can learn. Finally, they need access to elders, people who can offer them evaluation and advice. In simpler societies these learning resources are easy to come by in the natural course of living. In urbanized societies it may be necessary to make arrangements, for instance, by having a computerized service to help people locate the appropriate things, peers, models, and elders. But schools, according to Illich, only stand in the way, by controlling access to learning resources.

In this paper I want to carry forward the question Illich has raised: What do people need in order to learn? Instead of dealing with learning in general, however, I shall look at four different kinds of learning that seem to require different resources. Also, at the end I

Reprinted from the *Elementary School Journal* 73 (May 1973), 435-446, with permission of the author and the University of Chicago Press.

shall consider a question different from Illich's: Given the near certainty that the elementary schools will continue, whether or not they are necessary for learning, how can they best provide resources for the varieties of learning?

The following four kinds of learning will be the basis for most of the discussion in this paper: direct-application learning, basic skills, background knowledge, and personal learning.

1. Direct-application learning. When you learn a new sport or a job or a craft, you acquire knowledge and skills that are directly put to use in performing the sport, the job, or the craft. This kind of learning is merely an early stage of doing. It may be formally separated from practice, like driver training, but often it is indistinguishable from practice, as when you start in skating and gradually get better at it through nothing more than doing it.

2. Basic skills. Some kinds of practical learning are not directly applied. When you learn arithmetic, you do not begin to do arithmetic in the way that you begin to do knitting, having learned to knit. The activity of doing arithmetic is not pursued for its own sake or as a regular duty. What counts here is the capability of doing arithmetic rather than the doing itself. Basic skills may be very useful, but their use is more indefinite and remote than is the case with direct application learning. The main basic skills are the traditional three R's of the schoolroom.

3. Background knowledge. This is another kind of learning that is of indefinite or remote use. Premedical students are required to study chemistry and physiology. Such knowledge is not directly applied in medical practice, and it is difficult to specify its function at all. Yet knowledge of chemistry and physiology is thought to be useful to a medical person in a way that a knowledge of geology, for instance, would not be. We tend to speak of such knowledge not as being applicable to particular activities but rather as being relevant to them.

4. Personal learning. For a great deal of learning it makes no sense to speak of "using" it. This kind of learning is valued because of what is supposed to happen to the learner in the process—hence the name, *personal learning.* It includes any learning that is supposed to affect a person's character, tastes, mental abilities, and the like. Pure examples of this type are hard to find. Most learning experiences are chosen to produce side benefits in the form of useful knowledge and

SAINT PETER'S COLLEGE LIBRARY
JERSEY CITY, NEW JERSEY 07306

skills in addition to ameliorative effects on the personality of the learner. Psychotherapy often aims at pure personal learning, as do some educational programs aimed at making people creative. Should this sort of thing be called learning at all? Yes, even if it is difficult to specify what is learned. If we consider learning to be the residual effects of experience, then changes in traits, attitudes, and abilities may certainly be described as learning. Moreover, they are the central concern of many educators.

Real-life learning events do not in general fall into any one of these four categories. A school reading lesson, for instance, may teach reading through a selection that conveys potentially useful background knowledge in the context of a morally or aesthetically uplifting story. Yet it is useful to consider such a lesson in the light of the varieties of learning. Does the lesson serve them all? Is it replaceable? These categories also help us see where present emphases and actual needs lie. Obviously schools are concerned mainly with basic skills and background knowledge, the two categories of learning that are characterized by indefinite and remote application. This observation may help us understand the problems and the limitations of schools as learning resources.

Direct-application Learning

This is a natural kind of learning and is the kind most preferred by educational radicals. It is intimately tied to a desired activity and draws its motivation from it. One does not learn to dance because of a love of learning to dance, but because one wants to dance. Thus learning does not stand out as a separate activity that must have its own motivations and dynamics. This is not to say that direct-application learning is necessarily easy or pleasant. It may be arduous, frustrating, tedious, even painful. Most of these qualities are to be found in the first major piece of direct-application learning a child does— learning to walk. These qualities are found in such activities as learning to water ski, to roller-skate, or to speak a new language when one is an immigrant. People persevere in such learning because the activity is one they want to pursue. When a dismayed parent asks, "Why won't he work that hard to learn things at school?" the answer is not difficult to produce. The things taught in school are seldom tied, and seldom can be tied, to things the child wants to do.

Learning for direct application makes most sense when it is carried out in close association with the desired activity, in the same place and near to it in time. Torrance[2] found that knowledge about jungle survival took hold best when the lessons were carried out in a transport plane flying low above the jungle treetops. It makes little sense to learn, say, the practical procedures of computer programming if one is not going to have a chance to use the procedures for five years.

The general-purpose school is not appropriate for direct-application learning. In the world at large you learn a job on the job, you learn to ski at a ski resort, you learn to paint in a painter's studio. Learning facilities are fitted to the activities rather than the reverse. In school the problem is always to manufacture activities that can be fitted to the learning.

Another problem with centering direct-application learning in schools is that it becomes more remote from practice and begins to drift into the learning of basic skills and background knowledge. A school course in electricity, which may attract students who are eager to build radio sets or tricky photocell gadgets, drifts into a course of elementary knowledge about electricity and ends by boring students. The tendency for formal instruction to drift in the direction of teaching background knowledge is probably inevitable and is, I think, the basis of pedantry. Eventually the pedantry gets welded into the requirements of the activity itself, so that you cannot pass an examination for a carpenter's license without a lot of miscellaneous knowledge that has no direct application to carpentering and is at best relevant.

It is fairly obvious what learning facilities children need in order to pursue the activities they want to pursue. Children need playgrounds, gyms, museums, pools, and other athletic sites, as well as facilities that provide materials and places to meet for various hobbies, crafts, and performing arts. With all of these there should be such provisions for instruction as are needed, ranging from the most casual sort of helping hand to formal training in the more difficult skills. For children the main problems are ones of access. A kind of centralized school might help to deal with these problems.

The Learning of Basic Skills

The line between direct-application learning and the learning of basic skills is a difficult one to draw, but the difficulty is not entirely conceptual. There are differences in individuals and in situations that produce actual uncertainties. Consider learning to read. For some children this is clearly direct-application learning. They want to read. They catch on quickly and begin to read on their own and enjoy it. For them the learning phase, as distinguishable from merely reading and getting gradually better at it, is a matter of a few weeks (yet they will probably be subjected to six years of formal reading instruction). But there are other children, the majority I would guess, who learn to read by the age of seven but do not pursue it as an activity until years later, if indeed they ever read except on demand. Many academically capable boys do not begin reading voluntarily until they acquire a hobby around the age of ten or eleven and begin reading for information. Until then, they are not learning reading for direct application but for an indefinite and remote use.

The difference between children who read on their own early and children who do not has consequences. When reading is learned for direct application, reading provides the motivation for learning and also the kind of practice that efficiently promotes learning. When reading is learned as a basic skill, as something to have in one's repertoire, there are problems of motivation. The learning activities have to be rewarded or made entertaining. Continual practice must be provided, or the skill will decline. Children come back to school after summer vacation having forgotten how to read. The practice into which they are pressed tends to have a low yield. They go through the motions of reading, but they do not really care whether they are getting the message. Understandably, the learning is slow and unsteady.

What has been said of reading applies to writing, except that the number of children who pursue writing as an activity is much smaller. There are scarcely any children for whom writing is a case of direct-application learning. As for arithmetic, it is clearer yet that the reason for requiring mastery is not direct application. Arithmetic points up the difference between practice of a skill through desired activities and practice for skill through learning exercises. It is almost unbelievable that intelligent school children could take so long to learn so few computation skills so poorly as they do in our elementary schools, especially when you consider that street children in poor countries learn money arithmetic unerringly at an age when an American child cannot be trusted to add three and three.

An attractive solution to the problem of learning basic skills is to translate them into skills for direct application. Let boys wait until they are ten years old and want to read in connection with a hobby; and then do not teach reading in a school but have people at hobby centers, museums, and libraries whose job is to help children with reading. Whether a child was five or fifteen, he would be able to get competent training, but only what he needed for the reading he wanted to do. It would not be so easy as it sounds, but I have a hunch it would be a good deal easier and less expensive than what we do now. For a large number of children a couple of dozen hours of instruction at the right time would be all they would ever need in reading.

The weaknesses of this idea become apparent when we try applying it to writing and arithmetic. To be sure, the person who is ready to start work as a newspaper reporter or as an accountant but does not know how to write or figure is going to be an eager learner; but, of course, no such opportunities arise for the unskilled. You have to have the skills first, and the opportunities to use them follow. Furthermore, when specific needs for skills arise, it is generally too late to meet the need with learning. The illiterate who suddenly wants to write a letter to a senator or compare unit costs is not going to undertake the several years of study required to bring him to the point where he can do such things.

There is a reason why the three R's have gotten separated from other skills, to be taught in special institutions to children who often are not zealous to acquire them. These skills take a long time to learn well. If they are going to be available when you need them, you may have to start learning them years before the need is felt.

Reading may be a partial exception. As I have suggested, most children may discover a need to read while they are still young. But not all will do so, and few can be depended upon to discover a need to write or do arithmetic early in life. They will discover their need later in life, when it will be difficult for them to learn all they need.

Thus it appears that there is a need for formal training in basic skills. It should be available for all, even though not all will need it. It does not matter much whether such training is compulsory or optional by law; prevailing sentiment among parents would make the training compulsory for children. Such training, however, need not resemble present-day elementary schooling. It could be more like specialized training in athletic skills, with different trainers for different skills. It does not necessarily have to be scheduled daily, and it need not take up as much time as schools now devote to basic skills. It does not have to be so rigidly age-graded, and it can give children only what they need, as compared with the present system, which must give every child six years of something or other in every skill area.

One final question: Are there really no basic skills other than the traditional three R's? One could name a number of other communication skills and intellectual skills that might qualify as basic, but systematic training in them has not been developed and people seem to be getting along now on incidental learning of them. I see a possibility that systematic training will be developed in thinking skills—reasoning, idea production, inquiry, problem-solving, and the like—to the point where the effects are demonstrable and long range. If, as seems likely, such training had to be carried out over a number of years to become functional, then it is likely that the training would take its place with the three R's.

Another less basic skill, already on the scene, is foreign-language training. Everyone knows that foreign-language learning is most successful if it is learning for direct application—at its best if the learner is already involved with people who speak the language. By contrast, learning a foreign language as a basic skill for future use, as is done in schools, is dramatically unsuccessful. But what is a child in a monolingual environment to do? Formal language instruction accomplishes something. The only time when it is silly to teach a foreign language as a basic skill is when the opportunity exists to involve children in situations where they would want to learn the language for immediate use.

The Learning of Background Knowledge

Most of what has been said about basic skills applies to background knowledge. It is not needed for immediate use. It is, however, expected to be useful in various indefinite ways. A knowledge of history, it is thought, has some value in understanding and making decisions about current affairs. The values of a knowledge of history cannot be fully apparent while you are studying history, however, because you cannot know what the future holds. As with basic skills, it is worthwhile to acquire historical knowledge in advance of the occasion to apply it because history takes a good while to learn. But there is a more critical reason for possessing knowledge in advance. If you do not have it, you cannot know it is relevant. If you know nothing about city life in the Middle Ages, it cannot occur to you to investigate parallels between it and the way things are going in some American cities today.

You frequently hear these days that children do not need to acquire knowledge anymore but only the ability to use information-retrieval resources. The notion is utter nonsense. So is the notion that children do not need facts, but only general principles and models. It is usually among details that one discovers new relationships. It is as true now as it ever was that what distinguishes the educated man, what sets him off from the clever rustic, is his possession of a fund of background knowledge wide enough and functional enough that he can approach any new issue with some basis for intelligent judgment.

There are, however, serious difficulties in making provisions for the learning of background knowledge. The first is the question of what to learn. When the learning is for indefinite future use, one cannot know what knowledge will have the greatest applicability to future needs and events. One cannot even be sure how valid the knowledge acquired today will prove to be a decade from now (although again some modernists get carried away with the transitoriness of truth and are afraid to teach that the birds have wings lest someone come along tomorrow and prove they do not).

The three other major difficulties in the learning of background knowledge are psychological ones: they are problems of motivation, retention, and retrieval. "Why do we have to learn this stuff?" the surly child asks, and no answer you can give can be expected to satisfy him, much less charge him with zeal. Fortunately, human beings manifest curiosity, a desire to acquire knowledge and understanding in the absence of ulterior motives. But curiosity tends to be spotty and selective, fluctuating, easily stifled, and far from evenly distributed among human beings. Thus it is common to augment motivation for the learning of background knowledge by the use of social pressures, rewards, and by making the learning prerequisite to desired activities, for example, through licensing examinations or professional-school entrance requirements. Indeed, it is likely that the main motivation most students have for learning one thing is that they know it will be necessary for learning the next thing in the curriculum, an ersatz kind of direct-application learning that manages to keep the knowledge acquisition pot going at a very low simmer.

Retention is a horrendous problem in the learning of background knowledge. Background knowledge will not prove to be useful if it is forgotten, and most of what is learned is forgotten in a short time. A number of studies have indicated that about 80 percent of the facts learned in school subjects are forgotten within a year.[3] Apparently the rate of forgetting main ideas is much lower, although it is difficult to quantify memory for ideas in a way that makes comparison possible. However that may be, one cannot escape some sense of futility about pouring knowledge into the heads of children when it runs out so fast.

Often knowledge is not forgotten altogether, but the learner can retrieve it only by certain cues and in certain contexts. The person who will never think that water contains hydrogen and oxygen unless asked specifically, "What is the composition of water?" does not have a very useful piece of information in his head. Inert knowledge is what Whitehead called it. Functional fixedness and set are names for the corresponding psychological condition of inability to apply certain knowledge except on cue. Functional fixedness is found with knowledge learned for direct application as well, but in that case the knowledge at least has some significant function.

Much of what is most criticized in traditional schooling may be understood as a response to the special difficulties noted in the teaching of background knowledge. The set curriculum, specifying subject matter to be covered in each year, is a response to the question of what to learn; it is a response based on the not unreasonable premise that traditional and authoritative judgment is a better guide than childish interests in deciding what knowledge is likely to be of greatest future use. The system of assignments, tests, grades, and the emphasis on working hard and paying attention all begin to make sense if one recognizes them as a way of motivating children to acquire knowledge that is of no immediate use to them. The recitations, the reviews, and the tests are an answer to the problem of retention.

What has been the response of the school to the problem of retrieval? This is the greatest weakness of the traditional school. Because recitations and tests are the only occasions when children have to remember anything, they soon become the only occasions when children can remember any knowledge they have acquired at school. The result, of course, is inert knowledge, demonstrated by pupils who cannot apply a concept learned in one book to a problem in another. I do not think that schools have neglected retrieval problems out of ignorance, however. Everyone knows that knowledge should be made meaningful and available for use. The trouble is that when you have a fixed curriculum, taught through recitation and review, there is very little that can be done to promote flexible retrieval.

Miscellaneous vs. Structured Knowledge

The preceding examination of difficulties in teaching background knowledge might well suggest that the attempt should be abandoned and children left to their own devices. Children will acquire a fund of knowledge no matter what is done with them; the only concern is what knowledge they will acquire. Two worries stand in the way of leaving the acquisition of knowledge to children's own initiative: First, children may not acquire the "right" knowledge but may acquire instead knowledge that is worthless or incorrect. Second, the knowledge they acquire may be poorly organized, lacking in central ideas and logical structure.

Consider the knowledge in the better sort of school textbooks and ask, "Would children acquire such knowledge on their own?" It would take a true believer in Mother Nature to insist that they would or to insist that the knowledge they did acquire through their own initiative would be just as good. But the question is not a fair one because the knowledge in the book is not what children acquire from formal teaching. As we have noted, children forget most of what they are taught in the way of factual knowledge. It is not the knowledge in the book but some small, unspecified portion of it that is learned and retained. Most of what constitutes the fund of background knowledge that children carry with them into later life is going to be acquired from other sources anyway.

The second and more profound objection has to do with the structure of textbook knowledge. The knowledge embodied in a good textbook (and in a good informal or experience-based curriculum) is not just a collection of worthwhile facts. It has a structure that reflects the way the subject matter is understood by scholars in the field. Many an educator would argue that this structure is the most important thing for children to acquire. But are children capable of grasping the structure of a subject?

The question of what children are capable of understanding is a major one to consider in determining what provisions to make for acquiring knowledge. There is no point in making provisions for knowledge that children cannot acquire anyway. The curriculum reformers of the 1960's were optimistic about what children could understand.[4] This is curious because they generally took their psychological ideas from Piaget, whose work indicated that children below the age of adolescence could understand very little. They could not understand ratios or probability, for instance, without which not much of scientific theory is comprehensible. Piaget has held that preadolescent children are limited to operating with a logic of classes, and only at a more advanced stage are they able to deal logically with relations among propositions.[5] It is hard for me to imagine what the structure of a discipline might be if it does not involve relations among propositions. The neo-Piagetian work of Pascual-Leone[6] suggests that the basic intellectual limitation of children is in the number of schemes, rules, or ideas that they can handle simultaneously, a capacity that increases regularly with age. The big organizing ideas of disciplines—the "conceptual schemes," as one science curriculum project has called them—all integrate a number of schemes of lesser inclusiveness. Hence, it is not surprising that high-level organizing concepts like energy, adaptation, and equilibrium are beyond the children's reach, no matter how they are taught or what enlightening experiences the children are exposed to.

The conclusion I draw from these observations is that there is no use worrying about providing children with learning experiences that expose them to the structure of knowledge and the main ideas in various realms of inquiry, because the children will not understand them anyway. What, then, can they learn? Skills, certainly, and we have already discussed that. For children who show an interest in laboratory activities, there are many useful skills of the direct-application sort that they could learn. Also, they can learn facts, from general impressions, and grasp relationships between events.

These learnings, which add up to what I would call miscellaneous knowledge, are not to be treated as worthless. They are all that most of us possess in most fields of knowledge. A good example is what we learn from the daily newspaper. First we may note that we acquire a tremendous number of facts from our newspaper reading, but, like the schoolchild with his coursework, we easily forget 80 percent of them within a year. Does this mean that the activity is futile and might as well be abandoned? Not at all. There is a residue from the forgotten information. Unless we are serious thinkers about current affairs, the residue does not take the form of theoretical understanding or conceptual schemes. It takes the form of general impressions of what is going on in the world. These impressions are a useful form of knowledge. They are the basis of most of our judgments, and they help us perceive the relevance of future information that comes along.

This kind of knowledge, I claim, is what children acquire—not from reading, necessarily, but from television, talk, and firsthand experience. They retain a large miscellaneous collection of details, some factual, some false, imbedded in a lot of general impressions about how the world works. These impressions range from ones that are in accord with the best adult knowledge to ones that are grossly distorted or oversimplified. With children, however, the distortion and the oversimplification must be regarded as inevitable consequences of their cognitive limitations.

If we accept this unglorified view of children's capacities for the acquisition of knowledge, then I believe we can in good conscience abandon curriculum and teaching for background knowledge and leave knowledge acquisition to children's voluntary activities. What is needed, then, in the way of provisions for learning? Ample and attractive sources of information reasonably free of consistent bias. From these sources children could be expected to accumulate a large supply of information and to form impressions of greater or lesser validity about most matters of importance.

School, by its nature, is not a very good source of information for children. As a source of information the teacher is typically quite limited and often not reliable. Furthermore, the teacher's many other duties preclude full use of her as a source. Books, potentially a rich source of information, are not of much use for that purpose to most school-age children. Their low reading-comprehension abilities restrict them for the most part to getting the drift of narrative prose. Audiovisual media, which are more comprehensible to children, are expensive and complicated. They are likely to remain economically out of the reach of schools, except as token displays, so long as schools remain committed to teaching as their main and overwhelmingly costly function.

For the kind of miscellaneous knowledge that children are capable of, more promising information sources are broadcast television, do-it-yourself science museums, hobby clubs, and excursions. Formal teaching to impart knowledge to children is, I suspect, a historical accident. Such teaching can be effective with more mature learners. It can also be effective when used to teach skills. It was extended downward to children without much thought, as schools for children began to develop out of the medieval colleges. If we were starting elementary schools now for the first time, it is doubtful that anyone knowledgeable about children would support the unpromising notion of teaching children subjects like science, history, and geography.

My argument so far has dealt only with children. With adolescents and young adults it is a different story since a substantial number of them achieve a level of intellectual development that enables them to grasp bodies of knowledge in a mature way. They can profit from systematic study of a subject, working toward a high level of conceptual integration. Paul Goodman, generally opposed to formal education, recognized this fact and urged that every youth be exposed to intensive work in a discipline.[7] There is a question, however, as to how many people can ever profit from such work. Inhelder and Piaget[8] implied that every normal child eventually reaches the stage of formal logical operations, which equips him to pursue an intellectual discipline. More wide-ranging research, however, has suggested that perhaps no more than half of the population reaches this stage. As far as acquisition of knowledge is concerned, this means that half the people would be better off acquiring knowledge of the world in a miscellaneous, newspaper-reading fashion, gradually developing a slightly more sophisticated and accurate set of impressions about how the physical world, the ecosystem, society, the economy, and the human mind and the body function. That is all most of us have to go on in most areas anyway, and we do not feel discouragingly stupid because of it.

Personal Learning

When we turn to personal learning, we turn to the heart of educational purpose. Skills and knowledge are but the veneer. At bottom what counts is what a person is: his character, his values, the way his mind works, his personal style. Personal learning has been so much the subject of empty rhetoric that we are likely to forget that it actually does occur. Children who grow up in a given culture tend (with wide variations, of course) to acquire personal characteristics that mark them as belonging to that culture.

If we think only of the pathetic efforts at fostering personal learning that go on in our schools and our psychology laboratories, we might suspect that such learning is a myth. "You can't teach honesty" is a reasonable conclusion to draw from research on that topic and from an informal assessment of the perennial efforts of schools to foster honesty in pupils. Yet the world is full of honest people who somehow or other learned to be that way. It is ironic that schools, dedicated in principle to personal learning as their highest goal, have no evidence of accomplishment to show for their efforts. All they can really be credited with is teaching some skills and knowledge.

Yet there is no mystery about why schools have no visible impact on values, attitudes, personality traits, and mental abilities. Any of us could write a prescription for producing personal learning. To induce a certain trait—say orderliness or compassion—you have to raise the child in a social environment where this trait is continually demonstrated and integrated into the whole texture of life, where manifestations of it are consistently reinforced and where lapses from it are not reinforced, where other things that are learned are consistent with it, where it is made an explicit value about which strong feelings are expressed and engendered. In short, the trait must be a salient one in the immediate cultural environment of the child throughout his formative years.

There is no point in detailing the ways in which schools fall short of meeting these conditions for personal learning. They are simply not geared to the job. They can reinforce traits that are already salient in the cultural environment of children, but they cannot do any sort of job of their own in the face of contrary or nonsupportive influences on the outside.

Is it possible that personal learning could be induced in any deliberate fashion? Can the forces of the home environment be overridden? The world has seen powerful agencies of personal learning— monastic orders; the British public schools, perhaps; the Communist youth programs in Russia and China. The question is not can it be done, but can it be done in any way and to any end that we should truly want to see.

The question of providing for personal learning, thus, is a question of values. All I will do at this time is state my own position on the moral and the political issues involved. I think only the parents, and not the state, have a right to determine what traits of character and personality should be induced in a child. We may make exception in the case of the delinquent child who has proved himself a social menace, but we should certainly not make exception for whole socioeconomic or ethnic categories of people who are deemed to be in need of personal improvement.

The only general provisions for personal learning that I find morally acceptable are provisions for what might be broadly characterized as self-improvement. These would include counseling and psychotherapy—offered on a voluntary basis, of course. But they could also include forms of help for people who wanted to improve their physical fitness, their intellectual abilities, their tastes, or their habits in such matters as orderliness or inquisitiveness. I would think, however, that these should generally be provisions for adolescents and adults. For children there should be no formal provisions for personal learning except for children in serious need of therapy.

If the elementary school is to continue—and I think that institutional inertia, among other things, guarantees that the elementary school will continue—then it will be profitable to reconceive it, not as an institution with some defining purpose, but rather as a convenience. Its convenience lies in the fact that children need adults to look after them. This need is most easily met if children are looked after by the same adults in the same place most of the time. The school can provide convenient access to many of the various kinds of learning resources mentioned here.

A school can, first of all, be the site of a number of the activities—sports, athletics, hobbies, and the like—that children want to engage in and for which they need some directly applicable learning. In this regard the more active sort of YMCA is a better model than the school as we know it. There is more emphasis on the doing and less on the learning, and there is more diversity without the overarching presence of a program or an educational philosophy.

The elementary school could also serve as the home of some sources of information and as an organizer of travel to other sources of information. Here the open-plan school in its most open forms is a fair model, although in such schools there is often a lot of implicit curriculum and subtle prodding to learn that could be eliminated. Finally, the elementary school could house facilities for training in the three R's and such other kinds of basic skill training as might eventually prove valuable. I say house because it would not seem appropriate for such training to be carried out by the same people who were responsible for tending the children and for seeing them from place to place.[9]

The kind of school I have described sounds disunified. Perhaps it also sounds chaotic, but it should not be. An overall administrative plan, perhaps on the model of a summer camp with counselors continually responsible for small groups of children, could insure a sufficiently orderly life in school. But disunified it would be. There would not be a coherent purpose, such as the educational goal of "developing the whole child." The school would simply be the location of a variety of facilities and activities that were grouped together as a matter of convenience, necessity, or economy. Activities like health care and bicycle safety checks are already often tied to schools for such reasons. It would therefore be quite proper to drop the name *school,* with its connotations of educational purpose and coherent program, in favor of a more noncommittal name like *children's community center.*

Notes

1. I. Illich, *Deschooling Society* (New York: Harper and Row, Harrow Books Edition 1972).

2. E. P. Torrance and R. Mason, "Instructor Effort to Influence: An Experimental Evaluation of Six Approaches," *Journal of Educational Psychology* 49 (August 1958), 211-18.

3. L. J. Cronbach, *Educational Psychology* (New York: Harcourt, Brace, and World, 1963).

4. J. Bruner, *The Process of Education* (Cambridge, Mass.: Harvard University Press, 1960).

5. B. Inhelder and J. Piaget, *The Growth of Logical Thinking from Childhood to Adolescence* (New York: Basic Books, 1958).

6. J. Pascual-Leone. "A Mathematical Model for the Transition Rule in Piaget's Developmental Stages," *Acta Psychologica* 32 (August 1970), 301-45.

7. Paul Goodman, *The New Reformation* (New York: Random House, 1970).

8. Inhelder and Piaget, *op. cit.*

9. C. Bereiter, "Schools without Education," *Harvard Educational Review* 42 (August 1972), 390-413.

2. Processes, Problem Solving, and Curriculum Reform

Richard W. Burns and *Gary D. Brooks*

What are processes? What role should they play in education? How are they related to problem solving and other terms used with them? How can they influence curriculum reform at all levels of education?

Processes belong to a type of objective differing from the cognitive entities (knowledges, understandings, and skills), the affective entities (attitudes, interests, and appreciations), and heuristic entities (strategies). Processes, as a type of objective, are specific mental skills which are any of a set of actions, changes, treatments, or transformations of cognitive or affective entities used in a strategy in a special order to achieve the solution of a problem associated with the learning act, the use of learning products, or the communication of things learned. Processes are, more simply, transformational entities.

Processes are not new—they are the skills that learners have utilized since learning first occurred. Being a type of objective or end product, it is inaccurate to view them singly or collectively as a "method of instruction." Processes are complex skills which learners use in transforming knowledges and understandings in order to effect solutions to problems. They could also be called "problem-solving

Reprinted from *Educational Technology* 10 (May 1970), 10-13, with the permission of the authors and the publisher, Educational Technology Publications, Inc.

skills." Processes are the mental skills needed in any problem-solving situation associated with learning, using what has been learned, or communicating about things learned.

Examples of process terms are abundant. It is difficult, however, to be sure that a listing of processes is complete and that each process identified is "pure" (without overlap with another process). Much further research is needed to compile a comprehensive, valid, and clearly defined list of processes. The following list of terms is not comprehensive, but typifies what is meant by processes:

1. Abstracting	5. Evaluating	9. Simulating
2. Analyzing	6. Generalizing	10. Synthesizing
3. Classifying	7. Inferring	11. Theorizing
4. Equating	8. Sequencing	12. Translating

Each of these process terms is in reality a category name for a sub-group of synoptic or highly correlated terms. For example, *simulating* is also affecting, assuming, copying, counterfeiting, faking, imitating, making believe, mocking, pretending, and shaming.

To describe each process in detail and to list behaviors associated with each is beyond the scope of this essay. However, translating will be explained as an example.

Most behaviors associated with translating can be either oral or written, and the majority are also reversible. The outline below lists the main transformations a learner could make in translating. The term *symbol* refers to any character other than a word, and the term *verbal* refers to word symbols.

   I. Verbal to verbal
     A. One language to the same language
       1. Rewording—finding a synonym
       2. Converting to another form—poetry to prose
       3. Rewording—idiom to general language
       4. Rewording—simile to general language
       5. Rewording—metaphor to general language
       6. Abstracting (outlining)—lengthy to brief
       7. Abstracting—concrete to abstract
       8. Rephrasing—general language to general language
       9. Substituting—example one to example two

B. One language to another language
 1. Rewording—finding synonym
 2. Converting to another form—poetry to prose
 3. Rewording—idiom to general language
 4. Rewording—simile to general language
 5. Rewording—metaphor to general language
 6. Abstracting (outlining)—lengthy to brief
 7. Abstracting—concrete to abstract
II. Symbolic to verbal
 A. Symbol to word
 1. Converting—number to word
 2. Converting—abbreviations to words
 3. Converting—technical symbols to words
 B. Illustrations (two dimensional) to words
 1. Converting—drawings to words
 2. Converting—paintings to words
 3. Converting—photographs to words
 4. Converting—graphs to words
 C. Realia (three dimensional) to words
 1. Converting—object to words
 2. Converting—object system to words
III. Symbolic to symbolic
 A. Technical symbol to technical symbol
 1. Converting—number to number
 2. Converting—letter to letter
 3. Converting—color to number
 B. Symbolic to illustration
 1. Graphing—number to drawing
IV. Symbolic to performance
 A. Illustration (two dimensional) to performance
 1. Constructing—drawing (plan) to scale model
 2. Constructing—drawing (plan) to real object
 3. Converting—music to playing
V. Verbal to performance
 A. Words or letters to performance
 1. Converting—words to hand signals
 2. Interpreting—words to actions

How do processes relate to other educational end products?[1] If one refers to the cognitive entities as Type I objectives and the affective entities as Type II objectives, then processes are transformational entities, or Type III objectives. A fourth type of objective, heuristic entities, are called strategies. Processes are mental skills used in handling, dealing with, or transforming information, using the term broadly. Type I and Type II objectives are learned behaviors which can be thought of as input in a computer analogy, while the processes are the separate treatments applied to the input by the computer. The specific sequence of treatments is the program or the strategy. The output is the solution of the problem.

Information as knowledges (facts, dates, names, events, laws, low-order principles) and understandings (high-order principles, relationships, classifications, functions, etc.) are the major sources of input, but these are essentially sterile bits of information unless they can be related, compared, equated, generalized, ordered, and in other ways treated or transformed in what is generally called thinking or problem solving.

Expressions such as "he knows a lot but can't apply it," "he is smart enough but a poor teacher," "he knows it but can't explain it," indicate a common notion that learning can be less than functional. An interesting hypothesis is that the fault lies in the learner's failure to master process goals. Data, to be functional, must be manipulated and transformed by the thought processes previously listed as examples.

Processes and Strategies

Strategies should not be confused with processes. Strategies are high order heuristic principles which are used in devising or applying specific processes in a plan (used in a special order) to achieve a definable goal, such as in problem solving. Although strategies are learned and necessary in problem solving, which makes them important goals in education, it remains doubtful that they should be taught as such in the classroom. Learners in problem-solving situations will automatically learn strategies. Generally, strategies will be highly individualized. In devising plans for use in problem solving, each learner will find unique procedures which are effective. Uniqueness may be the result of trial and error, past learnings, lack of identifying an alternative, prior exposure to a particular method, habits, or other factors. Most problems do not have just one method of solution. Two individuals faced with the same problem, with access to identical data, and using the same material facilities, may reach identical conclusions by utilizing different strategies.

Formalized strategies occur with some frequency in mathematics. These strategies are taught and learned directly as objectives. In this same sense a computer program, after it is devised, becomes a formal strategy. The scientific method is merely a condensed and loose description of a general way of thinking; and, in practice, the method varies greatly with the problem to be solved and the human problem solver.

The term "process method" has no meaning, as processes are used in all strategies of problem solving. Gagné[2] describes the relationship between problem solving and discovery as one involving the presence or absence of a "verbally stated solution." Both problem solving without discovery (principle learning) and problem solving with discovery entail the use of instructions (aids to the learner). The difference lies in the fact that in principle learning the solution to the problem is given verbally, while in discovery learning the solution is never given verbally. In other words, problem solving and discovery are the same when a verbal solution is not given and the learner solves the problem by discovering.

Are processes and the teaching of processes the sole property of science education? Obviously not, as processes are used whenever and wherever problems are solved. Any curriculum and any subject learning can be process oriented.[3]

In summary, processes are learned, transformational entities which are used in learning and problem solving—regardless of the methods used and the subject matter considered. Using one or more processes in any order to solve a problem results in a strategy. Strategies may or may not be direct educational goals, due to their variety and uniqueness to the individual learner who applies them. A great deal more research is needed to validate processes and to define their total role in learning.

The Process Approach and Information Orientation

The first [article (in the same issue of *Educational Technology*)], "The Need for Curriculum Reform," detailed the futility of conceiving new curricula based on the traditional approach, which is essentially one of information orientation. Information-oriented curricula should be extensively re-evaluated in the light of current social-cultural trends and new insight into how people think and learn.

What is information orientation and why are curricula so oriented? Information orientation quite simply refers to subject matter content dealing with topics which are presented in such a way that learning becomes primarily a memorization process. Learners acquire bits of information, such as names of authors, painters, composers and inventors; assorted dates associated with discoveries, financial transactions, court rulings and battles; the names of the parts of animals, plants, machinery, grammar and speech, and thousands of other assorted facts. Currently students are being educated as if each was a type of memory drum—they are expected to store hundreds of thousands of bits of information in the fond hope that they will both need and recall such information at later times.

The effect of the modern "information explosion" has been to outmode any type of education conceived on the basis of information needed to effectively master "a single subject." Each historical subject is now more likely a field of study. For example, chemistry has grown from a single subject to several large fields of concentration, including physical chemistry, biochemistry, nuclear chemistry, and petroleum chemistry, each of which is a specialized area demanding several years of concentrated study.

Perhaps the very broad goals of education have not changed. These broad goals generally refer to the learner acquiring behaviors that will insure his becoming an effective, productive member of a family unit and an effective member of the society in which he lives. However, to achieve these goals today requires a new approach to education. No one operating in a complex social structure can be effective in that culture by merely attempting to assimilate facts.

An Alternative—A Process-oriented Curriculum

What is it that a person must do beyond acquiring information? The most obvious answer to this question is, "the person must think."

Today's living calls for problem-solving skills, concept formation skills, data-processing skills, the ability to make judgments and discriminate, the ability to relate causes to effects, the ability to analyze, the ability to summarize, and the ability to form valid conclusions. The cultivation of these general abilities is not and never will be the result of curricula which are solely information oriented. To develop behaviors associated with these abilities requires curricula which are specifically designed to achieve such ends. Curricula must be process oriented if the learners are to develop processing behaviors.

On the surface, it may appear that present-day curricula do teach thinking and problem solving. Many educators, especially school administrators, claim goals, aims, and objectives for school systems that in actual practice are not being achieved. High-sounding terms such as effective citizenship, the scientific method, creativity and problem solving are prominently displayed in lists of educational goals. Actually, the behaviors required of students are those that are measured in unit, semester, or final examinations. A recent analysis of fifty such tests in science and history reveals the true nature of what is often being expected of learners at the high school level. Each item on the teacher-made examinations was analyzed as to the type of objective it measured. A summary of the results revealed that 1,620 of 2,010 items (81 percent) were classified as measuring "knowledges" (facts and low-order information) exclusively. "Understanding" accounted for 219 items (11 percent) and 164 items (8 percent) were classified as measuring "skills." Less than 1 percent (7 items) were designed to measure "processes" or high-order mental skills. However, the goals reported by the teachers for the subjects covered by the fifty tests included research skills, problem-solving skills, reasoning, logical thinking, appreciations, and interpretation of research data.[4] It is extremely doubtful that these exemplary goals were being accomplished.

Further studies should be initiated comparing the actual achievement of learners with the types of objectives that can realistically be achieved.

Information would not be excluded from the new curriculum, but the amount would be reduced. Whereas information is now both the means and the end of instruction, it would in most instances be reduced to the role of means only. Information would provide the basic input—the grist—for the development of problem-solving skills. Problem solving, with and without discovery, would demand that learners develop skill in each of the processes named. These processes, in turn, when applied to further learning, using what has already been learned, and communicating about things learned would result in the learners' acquiring useful strategies.

Processes are extensively used in problem solving, and therefore it is reasonable to assume that one of the primary ways processes are acquired, developed, and become functional is through learning to solve problems.

What Is Problem Solving?

A problem exists for any learner when his present knowledges, understandings, skills, attitudes, appreciations, and interests are such that his behavior repertoire (what he can do) is incapable of finding a solution. If a problem exists, it may or may not be capable of being solved. If the learner has the appropriate recallable knowledges, rules, concepts, and principles needed for the solution, then it is highly likely that he can succeed. So, problem solving is in some sense having the appropriate background. This implies that a state of readiness is a necessary prerequisite. Problem solving implies that as the learner solves a problem he acquires a new behavior, which he adds to his behavior repertoire. In other words, at the end of the problem-solving sequence, the learner can do something he could not do before. Problem solving results in learning, and it is not merely a mechanical process. Some types of classroom activities are inappropriately called problem solving. Problem solving, in the sense used here, means that the learner acquires some new knowledge, rule, concept, or principle or that some new relationship between previously learned entities is discovered which allows him to demonstrate a terminal behavior that he did not have when he entered the problem-solving situation. *Unless learning occurs, there is no problem solving.*

Steps in Problem Solving

In problem solving, the first step can be described as problem recognition, which is marked by behaviors that are goal-oriented. If the learner is motivated to solve problems, his behavior will be sustained until a solution is found. In the classroom, problem solving is rarely associated with the reduction of primary drives (acquisition of food, water, air, physical security, sex). Most human motives are social in origin; and some, such as competition, vary in strength from one culture to another. Problem solving is therefore associated with social drives, such as success (achievement), mastery (excelling), approval (recognition, acceptance), and curiosity (excitement, adventure).

There is no absolute need that problems possess social usefulness, but the problems posed will more likely be solved if they are perceived as useful by the learner. By useful is meant relevant to the life of the learner, sensible and logical, and of immediate satisfaction. If problems meet these criteria, there is no guarantee that each learner will recognize the problem for what it is. Some needs may have to be developed by the learner prior to his being able to perceive or conceptualize the problem as one worthy of his consideration and effort.

Some problems may have high intrinsic interest, especially to learners who have developed motives associated with "learning for learning's sake." These students are definitely in the minority, but, because of their excellent learning skill, the problems they work on should be associated with individualized instruction in preference to their being offered to all groups. Other pupils may undertake the solution of problems merely for the sake of pleasing the teacher or to avoid adult disapproval and censure. Problems of this type—that have no other appeal—should be eliminated from curricular designs.

Problems, then, are perceived by individual learners generally to the degree that they appear to be significant. Problems perceived by teachers as having social utility may be rejected by learners because there is no immediate indication of a personal need—no immediate payoff. Teachers may pose problems for students as opposed to having students locate and identify them, but the problems so posed should be relevant to the students' lives, or possess high intrinsic interest to individual learners.

Finally, when are learners ready to work on a problem? A handy proof of readiness is the learner's ability to express the problem in his own terms. Failure to express a problem verbally or in writing indicates the learner's need for direction, which may be given by the teacher. Directions may aid the learner in locating, perceiving, and conceptualizing cues, and verbalizing the statement of the problem.

The second step in problem solving is conceptualizing the solution.

This step may be imperfectly formed, but the intended solution must be a reasonable enough model so that, when solution occurs, it is recognized as fulfilling the criteria for solution as posed by the problem. Gagné suggests that instructions as an external condition to learning may be given to inform the problem solver of the criteria for solution. In a sense, the problem solver conceptualizes a solution model, which he carries with him until the solution is accomplished.

The third step in problem solving is recall and selection of related information. No learner solves problems without first securing (learning) those rules, principles, concepts, and knowledges necessary for a problem's solution. This step in a sense is twofold: (1) recalling of information and (2) selecting those bits of information pertinent to the problem. These functions do not necessarily occur contiguously, nor completely. Recall and selection may continue throughout the problem-solving process, but obviously occur prior to the solution. Again, instructions may be given by the teacher to help direct the problem solver to recall or select relevant information.[5]

The fourth step in problem solving is hypothesis formulation. At this step the learner combines the rules, principles, concepts, and information which he selected in the third step. Obviously, many combinations are possible, and the learner does not always select the correct combination. In this sense, the hypothesis or hypotheses are only tentative. Effective problem solving quickly narrows the possible combinations down to one. Again, external instruction may be used which in effect both narrows the search for highly probable combinations and reduces the search time.[6]

The fifth step in problem solving is the formation and matching of the tentative solution. In the fourth step, the search for a tentative solution narrows the search until a highly probable combination of information is devised which will apparently fit the problem. In the fifth step, the tentative solution is then matched with the conceptualized solution from step two, which is recalled for the matching. If it appears that the tentative solution matches the conceptualized solution model, then the learner is ready to begin verification.

The sixth step is verification. At this point in problem solving, the learner applies the tentative solution from the fourth step to a problem instance (real example). Sometimes several examples are verified to be sure the solution "works." Should the solution not appear applicable, the learner generally returns to the fourth step, and selects another highly probable combination from the information he has recalled, enabling him to form a new tentative hypothesis concerning the solution. If the verification process is successful, then the solution has been validated.

Summary

In summary, present-day education places too much emphasis on the learner's memorization of information. Problem-solving skills are neglected, and the processes needed for problem solving are not receiving direct instructional attention. Curriculum reform efforts need to consider the inclusion of materials and activities associated with processes and aimed at learning objectives related to learner's abilities to solve problems, think and become independent in the pursuit of "understanding the world about them."

Notes

1. Richard W. Burns, "The Theory of Expressing Objectives," *Educational Technology* 7 (October 30, 1967), 1-3.

2. Robert M. Gagné, *The Conditions of Learning* (New York: Holt, Rinehart and Winston, Inc., 1966).

3. Richard W. Burns, "The Process Approach to Software Development," *Educational Technology* 9 (May 1969), 54-57.

4. Richard W. Burns, "Objectives and Content Validity of Tests," *Ibid.* (December 15, 1968), 17-18.

5. Benjamin Klinemuntz, *Problem Solving: Research Method and Theory* (New York: John Wiley and Sons, Inc., 1966) 36.

6. *Ibid.,* 141.

Selected References for the Cognitive Processes Orientation

Eulie, Joseph. "Developing Critical Thinking and Understanding Through the Social Studies," *Social Studies* 59 (October 1968), 216-21.

Rohwer, William D., Jr. "Prime Time for Education: Early Childhood or Adolescence?" *Harvard Educational Review* 41 (August 1971), 316-41.

Sarthory, J. A. "Law in the Public School Curriculum," *Social Studies* 61 (February 1970), 51-57.

Thomas, John I. "Concept Formation in Elementary School Social Studies," *Social Studies* 63 (March 1972), 110-16.

Part Two
Curriculum as Technology

The technological orientation to curriculum is one that is preoccupied with the development of means to achieve prespecified ends. Those working from this orientation tend to view schooling as a complex system that can be analyzed into its constituent components. The problem for the educator or educational technologist is to bring the system under control so that the goals it seeks to attain can be achieved.

Robert Gagné (Chapter 3) provides an excellent introduction to this conception of curricular problems. He identifies some of the hazards in the "hardware" aspects of educational technology and suggests what some of the more enduring contributions of curricular technology might be. Robert Silverman's description of the *S-R* model and its application to educational phenomena (Chapter 4) is a provocative overview of the theory and assumptions underlying the "technological" conception of curriculum. In Chapter 5, Goldman, Weber, and Noah provide an interpretation of curriculum as a response to the "supply and demand" factors influencing the educational enterprise. The technological orientation of the last of these chapters is revealed in the utilization of concepts and procedures drawn from the field of economics and applied in the field of education. The economic concepts and procedures serve not only as tools for resolving educational problems; they also define them. Thus we see the "nonneutral" consequences of the tools that are applied to deal with educational questions.

3. Educational Technology as Technique

Robert M. Gagné

When one hears or reads about technology and its effects on the instructional system, one is inclined to expect an immediate reference to large and flashy items of hardware, of which the best-known are closed-circuit television and the computer. And it is true that remarkable and highly visible changes in instruction can be readily seen in those "experimental" schools or classrooms where students busily take notes from a demonstration shown on television receivers, or where students in individual carrels type out answers to questions displayed to them on a tiny screen. But how accurate is such an image for the question of the effects of technology on instruction? Are we seeing the essence of the kinds of changes to be expected from technology, or only some superficial features of it? Is this a comprehensive picture of what technology means for instruction, or is it a very small and partial one?

My answers to these questions, which I want to expand upon here, are contained in the following statements:

This article is adapted from a paper delivered at the Eighth Annual Social Science Institute for Educational Administrators, Carmel, California, October 15, 1968, that appeared in *Educational Technology* 8 (November 15, 1968), 5-13. It is reprinted here with the permission of the author and the publisher, Educational Technology Publications, Inc.

1. Changes in instructional procedures are likely to be more profound than changes in hardware.

2. In many instances, small hardware changes instruction more than big hardware.

3. Hardware, small or big, sometimes makes possible instructional changes that are far-reaching in their effects; however, these depend upon the manner of use of the hardware.

Technology—Hardware or Techniques?

Some educational scholars have put forward the point of view that educational technology should not be equated to hardware. While it is perhaps easier for a lay person to understand "technology" as the use of machines in instruction, the more sophisticated use of the term is quite different.

Educational technology can be understood as meaning the development of a set of systematic techniques, and accompanying practical knowledge, for designing, testing, and operating schools as educational systems. Technology in this sense is educational engineering. It draws upon many disciplines, including those which design working space, like architecture; those which design equipment, like the physical sciences; those which design social environments, like sociology and anthropology; those which design administrative procedures, like the science of organizations; and those which design conditions for effective learning, like psychology. In technology, these disciplines are not pursued for their own sakes, but rather for the purpose of solving practical problems through the kinds of engineering efforts known as design and development. In connection with such efforts, there grows up a collection of know-how information, more or less generalizable to other problems in other settings, that deserves the name technology.

Technology seen in this way is a successor to common sense. People were using common sense when they designed educational films to be seen on large screens in auditoriums, just as they were in the movies; modern technology forces one to consider the specific functions of pictorial presentations in the process of learning. Common sense was also used in designing textbooks to contain prose sentences arranged in neat paragraphs on successive pages; modern technology, in considering the functions of texts in self-study, has already produced a considerable variety of ways in which printed information can be arranged and presented to the individual learner.

Technology seen in this way may or may not involve hardware. Sometimes it does; frequently it does not. It often involves changes in what "hardware people" call "software," which is a highly ambiguous term. Specifically, though, applications of modern technology often require the development of new kinds of student record cards, course outlines, study guides, lesson sheets, workbooks, teacher's manuals, and tests. Any or all of these may be needed to carry out new kinds of instructional procedures.

Consider now one of the changes this kind of technology has produced, and without any crucial degree of dependence on hardware development. The example is a genuine kind of individualized instruction, of the sort that is taking place in a suburb of Pittsburgh, under the leadership of the University of Pittsburgh's Learning Research and Development Center,[1] or in Philadelphia, or Monterey, or Duluth.

When a new class of children enters a new grade at Oakleaf School in Pittsburgh, they are given tests to determine what exactly they already know and what they do not know. The reason for such tests is that instruction designed for the individual student must start where he is as an individual—not where some abstract "average" student is. If the child already knows how to read unfamiliar words aloud, so be it; he will not be taught to do it over again.

This test and this procedure, which may be called "diagnostic placement testing," represents an important component of new technology. It is not something that already exists; it must be newly designed and evaluated.

The teacher, on the basis of facts about the child, then prescribes the child's first unit of instruction. The pupil, following these directions, goes to a materials center and gets a set of lesson units, which he then proceeds to work on by himself. They may contain, for example, several printed pages of exercises where the pupil matches sets of objects to numerals. Here is still another new development of technology. The materials center is unlike a library, in that it seldom contains large books; instead, it contains an enormous number of carefully classified lesson units. The units themselves need to be specially designed, for the pupil should do the work himself, ideally, without help from another person. Such instructional materials must obviously be addressed to the student, rather than to the teacher, and some technology is required to achieve this purpose. Sometimes a lesson unit may be a tape cartridge, rather than a printed sheet. Sometimes it may be a cartridge-type motion picture.

Suppose now that our new pupil has made some steady progress, and that he has completed an entire set of lesson units. Perhaps he has, by following the procedure described, brought himself to the point of being able to add small numbers by combining their sets. At a point such as this, another assessment is made of where he is, of how much he has learned, of where he is going next. Another kind of test assesses his ability to do all of the things he has learned to do, perhaps over a period of four weeks. This may be called a "phase test," and it, too, has to be specially developed as a part of technology. It is not something that exists as a standardized test. It is quite a different instrument, which is not oriented toward how pupil x compares with pupil y, but toward what student x learned in four weeks.

Having taken a phase test, our pupil now meets with his teacher. At this point, the teacher has a very critical job, and it must be done with as much precision and wisdom as possible. At this point the teacher needs something that may be called a "student progress record," which must be very detailed and very informative. It must do more than tell in general terms "how Tom is getting along." Instead, it must tell what precisely he has learned, what he has perhaps failed to learn, and the major alternatives open to him for further learning. Based on this record, and consultation with the pupil, the teacher can recommend for him a course of further study that will best suit his individual needs. Perhaps he needs to spend some time on the use of numbers in measurement, or in telling time; perhaps it is best for him to press on to the addition of larger numbers. The main point is that a student progress record of the sort required for these decisions is another kind of technological development that is necessary to carry out the purposes of individualized instruction. It is not a piece of hardware, obviously. But it must be designed and put into use with equal care.

Surely the techniques of individualized instruction must be counted among the most promising for educational improvement on the present educational scene. It is of considerable significance to note that this kind of educational change is mainly implemented by what is called software rather than hardware. It requires the development of new tests and diagnostic procedures, new kinds of lesson units that are not books, new kinds of materials centers that are not libraries in any traditional sense, new kinds of techniques to assess student progress, and new kinds of records of students' past and present performance. All of these fall into the category of new technology, yet most of them are not hardware.

Hardware may be used to implement some of these procedures, although it does not originate them. Sometimes the student uses a cartridge tape recorder, or a small movie projector—hardly novelties! The materials center may require narrow bins to hold lesson units, rather than wide bookshelves. To add flexibility, mobile carts may be used to transport instructional materials from one place to another. Individual student study stations may be of some use, in place of student desks. But in all these instances, hardware is at the service of the new procedures, rather than the other way around. As the practice of individualized instruction proceeds, a use may even be found for the computer—perhaps to store the mounting details of student records and to make them readily accessible, or perhaps to identify students who are at the same point in instruction so that group classes can be scheduled. In such instances, obviously, even the computer would be entirely subordinate to the instructional procedures. Software technology would dominate the hardware.

It is greatly to the credit of the University of Pittsburgh Center and of other groups that are trying these techniques that they have resisted the seductions of hardware from the beginning. All of these useful and important techniques of individualized instruction, all of this technology, were developed to perform certain functions without giving primary consideration to hardware. Now that development has proceeded to a certain point, the specific uses of particular kinds of hardware are becoming increasingly apparent. But it seems doubtful that this point would have been arrived at this soon, had they started with hardware.

Practical educational procedures seem a fruitful way to consider what educational technology really amounts to.

Small Hardware or Large Hardware?

The magnitude of educational change does not seem closely related to the size of the hardware used. Sometimes, a very small kind of hardware, or even a small kind of software, can bring about far more profound and far more desirable changes than the installation of large hardware. Perhaps the major reason for this is that the individual student, the learner, is the focus for change. Whatever large installation one may think about, the difference is going to be made where the student is. And it needs to be remembered that the student can only attend to one thing at a time—one might say, to one *small* thing at a time.

One kind of large hardware that has attracted considerable attention is the installation of television. Many carefully conducted studies[2] show that it is feasible to present almost any kind of instruction via television. There are studies[3] showing that students often learn as much from listening to a televised lecture as from listening to a live lecture. But, so far as I can tell, there are no studies showing that students learn more from television than they do from an equally well-planned alternative type of presentation. Chu and Schramm point out a variety of situations where televised instruction has been of tremendous value, particularly when there is a need to instruct large numbers of people in simple procedures in a short period of time.

These authors also point out, however, that, to be most effective, television needs to be used in a suitable context of activities at the receiving end. In other words, one must get back to the question of what the individual student is doing. This report also makes it quite clear, as other reviewers have noted,[4] that no special instructional value has been found in any of a wide variety of physical variables inherent to the medium—magnification, color, subtitles, viewing angle, repetition of scenes, or others. A lecture via television may indeed be presented in the same form to many students, but it is still a lecture. Its value for learning is dependent upon whatever effectiveness is in the lecture, and not because it is on television.

A second form of large hardware is the computer. Now, it is true that, if one is determined to use a computer as an instructional device, its characteristics and capacities make one want to strive mightily to use it efficiently. It is enormously expensive, and one doesn't want to be accused of using it merely to turn pages, as an automatic filmstrip projector does or as a student himself can do. Consequently, among those who explore computer uses in education, there is great concern to use its capacity to treat each student independently. In writing about this kind of usage, for example, both Suppes[5] and Bushnell[6] emphasize the use of the computer to make individualized instruction possible.

It is noteworthy, however, that some of the most prominent and so far successful tryouts of individualized instruction in this country have been started and carried on without computers. The procedures of instruction these pioneers have developed for use do not demand computers, although, as I have previously noted, they may arrive at a point where they perceive a possible usefulness for computers.

There are, as Suppes notes,[7] many problems to be solved before computers can progress from what he calls the "drill-and-practice stage" to the "tutorial stage" to the stage of "dialogue" in which student and computer interact freely with questions and answers. Now surely the "drill-and-practice" mode cannot be counted as a great educational innovation. Nor can this be said of the "tutorial" mode, which is formally similar in function to the branching programmed textbook. Accordingly, it may be seen that the great promise of the computer, as yet only partially realized, resides fundamentally in the development of software technology, that is, the development of instructional materials, which has not yet been achieved to any substantial degree.

I should not wish to be misunderstood, even at this point, about something my later remarks will clarify. I do not disparage the promise of the computer, and I firmly believe that studies of its educational uses are needed and worthwhile. I simply wish to point out that, at this point in time, just as is true of closed-circuit television, nothing about its inherent hardware characteristics has made possible any marked improvement in the effectiveness of instruction.

Contrast this record with the effects of some small items of technology. One of the clearest examples, in hardware form, is the eight-millimeter cartridge-loading projector. The effects of this device seem to me to be enormous, and by no means fully realized yet. Rather than arranging with the audiovisual department for the showing of a movie, with all the advance planning and logistical arrangements that usually requires, the teacher, or the student, is able to gain the instruction needed by a very simple procedure.

The major effect of this device, as I see it, is to put the audiovisual device where it must be for greatest effectiveness—at the service of the individual learner. The "concept film" does not try to present an entire lesson; rather, it presents that individual portion of a lesson that can be most effectively shown as a moving picture and leaves other portions of the lesson for other instructional procedures. In other words, it attempts to do in instruction only what it can do best.

My estimate would be that the availability of this small device has transformed instruction in a major way. It has encouraged, even forced, teachers to plan lessons in the kind of detail necessary for good instruction. Lessons must now be planned, not simply as major topics like "the evolution of vertebrates," to be shown on a film. They must now be planned so that the picture showing, which may be something like "contrasting nervous systems of the starfish and the perch," performs a specific function within a larger context. As a consequence, it seems to me that lesson design has inevitably become more precise, more realistic, more highly specified, and, as a consequence, probably more effective.

A second example of a "small" item of technology is the programmed instructional text, which may or may not be a part of a teaching machine. It is not my intention here to review all of the characteristics programmed instruction has, all of its good and bad features, all of its pros and cons. Instead, I want to point out what I think is a profound effect this movement has already had upon instructional practice, and which it continues to have.

From the beginning, designers and advocates of programmed instruction were faced with a difficult question posed by its critics: why was it better to learn from a program than to learn from reading a text? The answer has perhaps never been given in a direct manner. Instead, advocates of programmed instruction tended either to give abstract theoretical answers (like "immediate reinforcement") or to cite references to studies showing that programmed instruction really did work.

In facing the problem of making a program better than a text-book, the designers of programmed instruction came to emphasize the importance of objectives.[8] While it was difficult to say what objective, say, a chapter in a history book had, the programmed instruction people insisted that their form of instruction had performance objectives and that students could be shown how to achieve them. An objective came to mean something that the student was able to do. This was extremely important, and it will ultimately be involved, if it is not already, in demonstrating how effective an instructional device a history textbook really is.

What seems to me to be the most important lesson to have come from programmed instruction is, very simply, that instruction must be designed to teach the student the capability of doing something, not of "knowing" something. The notion of performance objectives is important because it emphasizes the doing. What is being taught is an intellectual skill, not recallable verbal information. To use other terms familiar to curriculum designers, the primary purpose of instruction is *process* not *content*.

The idea that the major and primary purpose of instruction is to teach processes, or intellectual skills, rather than verbal information, is, of course, not a new idea. It is reflected in statements of educational goals that say, in effect, that the purpose of education is to teach students to think. But either no one took this quite seriously, or, more likely, they lacked the techniques to make such an aim possible. I believe that the programmed instruction movement has pointed the way, and has actually developed the basic techniques, which make such an aim feasible. An educational trend which has been widely accused of emphasizing routine drill has in fact emphasized the one theme that points the way out of the dreary wilderness of empty verbalization—the emphasis on what the student can do.

The process emphasis in curricula, as it is seen in science, in mathematics, in social science, and even, to an increasing extent, in language arts, is, I think, an exceedingly profound change in the concept of what is to be learned. It is of far greater importance for educational effectiveness than the widely publicized "new" curricula where contributions mainly amount to an updating of theoretical viewpoints of the various disciplines. In science, for example, it is of undoubted importance to introduce the student to modern conceptions of the structure of matter. But it is of much greater educational importance to recognize and pursue the possibility that the student can learn to carry out the operations of a scientist—can learn, in other words, to view the world as a scientist does. The latter is what is meant by a "process objective," and it results from facing up directly to the question of what the student is able to do.

It seems to me that this orientation toward intellectual skills—toward what the student is able to perform, rather than what he "knows"—is an extremely important result of developing educational technology. But it must be noted that this result has not been achieved through hardware as such. Instead, it has been the systematic development of procedures and techniques of instruction, based on psychological theory. Sometimes it has involved such small hardware as teaching machines, and sometimes it has proceeded without the hardware, as in the case of programmed texts. Accordingly, I count this as an outstanding example of how technology—not large hardware—can have extremely far-reaching effects in the improvement of educational practice.

Some Effects of Hardware

As is well known, people are attracted to hardware more emotionally than rationally. They think that television is a marvelous invention; therefore it is bound to have great usefulness in education. Computers are great machines; therefore they must be useful for instruction. When any new hardware becomes available, people seize upon it with great enthusiasm, and they proceed to apply it to a practical area of social concern based on only the flimsiest of rationales. In the case of instruction, a case could be made that this happened with television, and it is happening with computers.

The results of such headlong application are by no means all bad. What seems to occur is that, in the course of trying hard to employ a new piece of hardware efficiently (in order not to be accused of irrationality), developers who have taken this approach more often than not discover some things of value. They find some new techniques, some new technology, which, while it is not hardware technology at all, nevertheless turns out to be valuable.

A number of examples of this tendency could be given. Some—the necessity for careful planning of televised lectures, the necessity for detailed specification of the functions of visual presentations in the use of cartridge-loading projectors, the necessity for defining performance objectives for instructional materials presented via teaching machines—have already been mentioned. Similar examples can be found in connection with attempts to use large hardware to solve instructional problems.

One such example comes from the employment of computers in connection with problem-solving games—in other words, the use of computers as "simulators." Simulation of "real problems" as an element in instruction has suffered some neglect over a period of many years. Perhaps this has been partly attributable to the prevailing prejudice for "purity" in education, and the consequent distrust of curricular components that partake of the practical. Simulation, however, is something that the computer is well designed to do. Consequently, the notion that computers can be used to provide practice for the student in solving problems that simulate real situations is very appealing.[9] A mathematics student can practice in a simulated sense what happens to a graph of a function if the value of a parameter changes. A chemistry student can perform simulated practice of a problem in qualitative analysis. Groups of students can carry out simulated practice of what happens when certain political or social decisions are made. The possibilities are nearly endless.

It may be noted, however, that simulation as a means of instruction does not absolutely require big hardware. The games of "Monopoly" and "Careers" are simulations that utilize very simple equipment. And many educational games, particularly those demanding social interaction, are still largely carried out without the help of major items of hardware. But computers exhibit many of the characteristics that make simulation easy and the efficient use of such expensive hardware possible. What seems to have happened, therefore, is that simulation exercises, since they are readily done on the computer, have become one of the most promising types of instructional uses to which computers are put. Thus the employment of computers has produced a kind of "forced by-product" of increased usage of simulation as an instructional technique. Few would want to say that this is anything but a fortunate outcome.

Consider another example, also involving the computer. In France a group studying instructional uses of computers[10] has come up with the following set of ideas: They wanted to use the computer to respond to the kind of answers made by a learner to questions on a test given after the study of a text. Up to now, the responses of a computer to such responses, or student errors, have been limited. The computer can presently respond to an overly long response time or to an error made by choosing a wrong item or typing a wrong word, which imposes great limitations on the use of the computer in instruction. It is one thing that makes Suppes' tutorial and dialogue modes so difficult to achieve.

The French investigators intend to get around this difficulty by analyzing what the learner has learned in terms of essential content. They will then place this content in the computer in the form of a glossary containing all the possible words the student might use in answering questions about what he has learned. To do this, it has been necessary to analyze the content in terms of its formal characteristics, in what seems to me to be quite a novel way. Briefly, they seem to be saying that the content of any subject matter is composed of two major classes of entities—concepts and relations. A subject like colloid chemistry, for example, can be described as a set of concepts (chemical structures) and relations among them. The number of concepts is, of course, a finite number; the number of relations, they contend, is also finite.

I mention this because it seems to me an outstanding example of how the determination to use big hardware can lead to a most remarkable sort of technological development that is not hardware at all.

Suppose it were possible to make a formal analysis of any subject matter to be taught in terms of a limited number of concepts and relations. It seems to me that this opens up marvelous technological possibilities for instruction. If we want to teach colloid chemistry, we first make an analysis of the subject to identify its concepts and its relations precisely. We then determine, by some experimental studies, how these can be most efficiently presented in a sequence. This provides a way of insuring that we know exactly, not merely in approximate terms, when the subject has been covered, and the degree to which the student has learned it.

A way is also provided to answer this last question about student learning by devising achievement tests which are in the best tradition of criterion-referenced measurement. Having a set of concepts and a set of relations, one can take a representative sample of both entities and assess student performance in terms of how many he knows, or in other words "how much" he knows. There is no need to depend upon the norm provided by what other students can achieve. If there are, in any defined subject matter area, 127 concepts and 14 possible kinds of relations, we immediately have a way of determining how much any individual student knows.

Out of the attempt to use a computer efficiently for instruction,

there has come the possibility of three important kinds of technological development: a way of defining in formal terms what is the
structure and substance of any subject to be taught; a way of determining effective sequences of instruction as patterns of concepts and
relations; and a way of assessing the outcome of student learning
against some specific and measurable criteria. Actually, such technology has not been fully developed as yet. But clearly, these are the
potentialities generated by using the computer in this way.

Conclusion

How can the practicing educator view the advance of technology
and its implications for instruction in the schools? My answer to this
question is that the most important elements of educational improvement are to be found in the technology represented by procedures of
instruction, techniques of instruction, and the systematic knowledge
associated with them.

Sometimes new instructional techniques make their appearance in
connection with small hardware, like easy-to-use projectors and tape
recorders. Sometimes they appear in association with large hardware
like television and computers. On still other occasions, the "things"
in which new techniques are embodied are as "soft" as printed pages.
Clearest in rationale are those instances where tryouts of new procedures generate the requirements for devices or equipment.

I have described examples to illustrate the point that procedures,
rather than hardware, are likely to represent the essence of change in
the relationship between learner and environment that we call "instruction." Sometimes these changes arise out of the use of small
hardware, sometimes out of large, but there seems to be no direct
relation between the size of the hardware and the size of the change.

I believe that new hardware, large and small, as well as new software, is going to bring about changes in instruction. Often, for reasons that appear difficult to understand, the tryout and use of hardware brings about changes that seem difficult to effect in other ways.
For example, educators have presumably been trying to individualize
instruction for many years without much change in what has actually
happened in classrooms. Will the lure of the computer actually
"force" a change to individualized instruction since it is hard to
conceive of using a computer efficiently in any other instructional

manner? Probably. If it does happen this way, though, the important changes will be seen to reside in the procedures and techniques of instruction. We will be using what is essentially an old machine to do a new job. What will be new about it will be the detailed procedure by means of which communication is established between the learner and his environment.

Notes

1. R. Glaser, "Adapting the Elementary School Curriculum to Individual Performance," Preprint 26 (Pittsburgh, Pennsylvania: University of Pittsburgh, Learning Research and Development Center, 1967).

2. C. R. Carpenter and L. P. Greenhill, *Instructional Television Research Report Number Two: The Academic Years 1955-56 and 1956-57* (University Park, Pennsylvania: Pennsylvania State University, 1958).

3. G. C. Chu and W. Schramm, *Learning from Television: What the Research Says* (Stanford, California: Institute for Communication Research, Stanford University, 1967).

4. A. A. Lumsdaine and M. A. May, "Mass Communication and Educational Media," *Annual Review of Psychology, 16* (Palo Alto: Annual Reviews, Inc., 1965), 475-534.

5. P. Suppes, "On Using Computers to Individualize Instruction," in D. D. Bushnell and D. W. Allen (eds.), *The Computer in American Education* (New York: Wiley, 1967), 11-24.

6. D. D. Bushnell, "Applications of Computer Technology to the Improvement of Learning," in D. D. Bushnell and D. W. Allen (eds.), *op. cit,* 59-67.

7. Suppes, *op. cit.*

8. R. Glaser (ed.), *Teaching Machines and Programmed Learning II: Data and Directions* (Washington, D. C.: National Education Association, 1965).

9. D. D. Bushnell, *op. cit.*

10. Personal communication from Dr. Jean Donio.

4. Using the S-R Reinforcement Model

Robert E. Silverman

I have previously stated that behavior-science models can be a basis for a technology of instruction in that such models can assist in translating principles derived from laboratory studies of learning into principles of teaching (*Educational Technology* [April 15, 1966, and October 15, 1967]).

The purpose of this article is to depict how one model, the *S-R* reinforcement model, can be used in designing an instructional plan. The model will be described and then its use will be illustrated in terms of the problem of teaching ninth-grade students the metric system for measuring length.

The Model

The *S-R* reinforcement model consists of a particular form of behavioral analysis in which behavior is represented in terms of the association between stimuli (*S*) and responses (*R*), and learning is represented in terms of the systematic changes in *S-R* associations

Reprinted from *Educational Technology* 8 (March 15, 1968), 3-12, with permission of the author and the publisher, Educational Technology Publications, Inc.

that occur when reinforcements are appropriately correlated with responses. The term reinforcement refers to the events that strengthen responses.

A positive reinforcer is any event that increases the likelihood of the responses that lead to it. Food, money, praise, a smile, getting a gadget to work are all examples of possible positive reinforcers.

A negative reinforcer is any event whose termination will strengthen behavior. The reduction of pain or discomfort is negatively reinforcing. A person will generally learn to make responses that enable him to escape discomfort or the threat of discomfort. Thus, escape from the threat of punishment is negatively reinforcing.

It should be noted that the term reinforcement is a general one including in its meaning the concept of reward, for rewards are positive reinforcers.

The *S-R* reinforcement model leads to an analysis of instruction in terms of certain fundamental factors in learning. The model calls attention to responses, reinforcements, and stimuli, and in so doing it indicates three essentials for learning: (1) The learner must make the response he is to learn. He learns what he does. (2) The responses must be strengthened. Learning progresses as the responses in question are reinforced and increase in probability. (3) The responses should be put under the control of particular stimuli; these stimuli will set the occasion for the occurrence of the responses.

It is of little value for a student to learn the name Napoleon Bonaparte unless he can give the response in the presence of such relevant stimuli as—"Who was the powerful Emperor of France during the first decade of the nineteenth century?" The question, in this case, is the stimulus that sets the occasion for the response.

The essential conditions of learning indicated by the model give rise to particular questions, and it is the answers to these questions that help in the solution of an instructional problem. The kinds of questions generated by the model are presented below. The questions are classified in terms of their relationship to response, reinforcement, and stimulus factors.

Responses

1. What are the responses to be learned? The identification of the responses is crucial if the teaching processes are to be effective. The learner acquires the behavior that happens to be occurring when reinforcement is given, whether or not this is the behavior that the teacher is trying to strengthen.

If many of the learner's responses are inappropriate, care must be taken to reinforce selectively only those responses that are deemed appropriate. The fact that the human is verbal and that much of his behavior is covert complicates the question, but it does not prevent its being answered. The best approach is to require as much overt activity as possible.

2. Are the responses to be learned already in the learner's reper-toire of responses, or are they novel and unfamiliar responses? For example, if the student is to learn to identify and label a diagram of the human eye, he must be able to use the appropriate technical terms such as cornea, iris, lens, conjunctiva, retina, etc. Where the terms are unfamiliar, prior experience with them in the form of familiarization practice will be helpful.

The model does not directly indicate techniques for solving such problems as familiarization training. It serves more as a tool of analysis rather than a producer of techniques. However, the emphasis on response, reinforcement, and stimulus does point the way to possible techniques, some of which will be discussed below.

3. What are the best ways to get the appropriate responses to occur? A basic condition of teaching is to ensure the occurrence of the appropriate responses. Very often the appropriate responses are evoked by direct guidance or prompting, the so-called "tell-and-do" method. In some fashion, the learner is shown how to make the response.

For example, his hand may be guided by the teacher as he prints a letter, or he is given the problem with the answer and asked to copy it, or he is given the rules for solving the problem and then required to solve it, and so forth.

A less direct but sometimes more effective method of getting the responses to occur involves allowing the learner to respond freely in a setting designed to encourage the appropriate responses and selectively rewarding approximations of the correct responses as they occur.

For example, in teaching a child to say a new word such as "brother" the child is encouraged to make vocal responses. Each time he makes a response approximating the sound of "brother" he is rewarded. The standard for reward is gradually raised, and by successive approximations the child is taught to say the word properly. Of course, the process can be shortened by providing the child with guidance in the form of a model to imitate. In that way the probability of his making appropriate vocal sounds is increased.

4. *What responses might compete with the responses to be learned?* The model indicates that competition among responses will retard learning. If two or more responses share a situation, the likelihood of any one of them occurring is consequently reduced.

For example, an English-speaking person learning to speak French has in his repertoire many pronunciation responses that compete with correct French pronunciation. Such a person often must suppress certain well-established responses in order to pronounce a word like *Saint-Cloud.* His initial tendency is to say "sant klaud," and it is only with difficulty he learns to substitute the correct pronunciation, "san klu."

5. *What can be done to reduce the probability of competing responses?* A simple answer to this question is to prevent competing responses from occurring. This may be done by providing sufficient guidance to evoke only the appropriate responses and then selectively reinforcing these responses. In certain kinds of learning situations that is good advice. But very often guidance is not sufficient, particularly when the competing responses are very strong.

When competing responses are strong, they must be extinguished and replaced by the appropriate responses. The process of extinction involves withholding reinforcement. The presentation of reinforcement makes responses more likely to occur, while the withholding of reinforcement extinguishes them, that is, makes them less likely to occur.

In the example above dealing with the pronunciation of Saint-Cloud, extinguishing the wrong responses would entail having the student respond to the printed words in such a way that each time he said "san klu" he would be rewarded, and each time he gave the English pronunciation, reward would be withheld.

Another approach would be to punish competing responses. For example, when Saint Cloud is mispronounced, the student is punished, and, when it is correctly pronounced, he is rewarded. If punishment is to be an effective suppressor, it must be strong. However, strong punishment introduces undesirable factors into a learning situation, often making the situation aversive by evoking emotional responses that may in turn provide another source of competing responses.

Reinforcement

1. What reinforcers will effectively strengthen the responses to be learned? The practical management of learning involves controlling reinforcing events, for these events play a critical role in determining whether or not a response will increase in frequency. While a major feature of the model is the principle of reinforcement, the model does not identify reinforcers for us. Many of these are well known and others can be identified by systematic observation.

We do know that praise, knowledge of having made a correct response, certain tangible items and particular symbols do prove to be effective reinforcers in a variety of teaching-learning situations. The effectiveness of each of these may vary from situation to situation and from learner to learner, but in general one of these or some combination will reinforce responses.

2. How can reinforcers be most effectively used? The model does tell us how to use reinforcers effectively and how to increase the effectiveness of reinforcing events by identifying three factors:

(a) The Delay of Reinforcement. Reinforcers are most effective when they are given immediately. Learning will be grossly retarded, or will not occur at all, if the learner is not reinforced at the time he makes the correct response. If reinforcement is delayed, some responses other than the correct one may be reinforced.

Teaching machines and programmed instruction were developed to provide an effective means for the immediate presentation of reinforcement. One of the key features of programmed instruction is the immediate feedback given to the learner. If the feedback informs the learner that he is responding correctly, it serves as positive reinforcement, increasing the likelihood he will make that particular response again under the same circumstances.

(b) The Quantity of Reinforcement. The quantity factor is related to the question of motivation. The incentive value of a reinforcer depends on the learner's experience with the reinforcer in question. For a positive reinforcer to have a high incentive value, the learner must have had ample experience being reinforced by it and at the time of learning be deprived of it.

A small quantity of reward can be very effective if the learner has experienced such rewards and is now deprived of them, while a large reward can be ineffective if the learner has been satiated with the reward. Mild praise can be strongly reinforcing to a student whose failures have been outnumbering his successes, while high praise may be ineffective for a student who is constantly achieving honors.

(c) The Frequency and Schedule of Reinforcement. The frequency with which a response is reinforced determines, in part, how well the response will be learned. In the early stages of learning, every correct response should be immediately reinforced. However, as the responses gain strength, they can be reinforced intermittently: Some of the correct responses are reinforced, and others are not. When this procedure is carefully followed, it is possible to maintain responses at a high strength by reinforcing them occasionally. Intermittent reinforcement schedules generally lead to a high rate of responding once the response is well established. Furthermore, responses that have been maintained on an intermittent schedule show greater resistance to extinction than responses that have been continuously reinforced.

Stimuli

1. What stimuli are to control the responses? Another way to put this question is: What discriminations must the learner make in order to respond appropriately?

It is necessary to identify responses in order to teach them, and it is necessary to identify stimuli precisely in order to associate them with particular responses. If a learning task requires students to do something in response to an auditory signal, the characteristics of the signal must be considered and care must be taken to ensure that the signal is actually a stimulus. In other words, a signal is a stimulus only when it is apprehended. An auditory signal that is not heard does not stimulate a response; a visual cue that cannot be seen serves no stimulus function; a question that is not understood cannot stimulate the response of answering.

2. How should stimuli be associated with responses? Teaching discrimination requires careful observation of the attention-provoking features of stimuli. The stimuli must capture the learner's attention if he is to learn to associate them with particular responses.

The actual association is carried out by pairing a particular stimulus with a response in the presence of some form of reinforcement. When this is done, the stimulus comes to set the occasion for the response, that is, it informs the learner that it is time to make a particular response and to be reinforced by doing so.

For example, a student learns to associate Pierre with North Dakota and Bismarck with South Dakota by first being reinforced for making the response "Pierre" to the stimulus, "What is the capital of North Dakota?" The question is the stimulus that sets the occasion for the response, and the correct response is, in turn, reinforced. An incorrect response, for example, "Bismarck," is not reinforced. The response of saying "Bismarck" to South Dakota is learned in a similar manner; it is reinforced in the presence of the question about the capital of South Dakota.

The key to discrimination learning involves the pairing of a stimulus with a response and seeing to it that the association of the particular stimulus and response leads to reinforcement. The stimulus in question is referred to as a discriminative stimulus. The question, "What is the capital of North Dakota?" is a discriminative stimulus for the response, "Pierre"; the question, "What is the speed of sound in air?" is a discriminative stimulus for the response, "1,100 feet per second"; and so forth.

3. How can potentially interfering stimuli be controlled? The best way to reduce interference from other stimuli is to arrange the conditions of learning in a setting that is as free as possible from distracting or interfering events. However, this may be difficult or impossible to do, particularly when the source of interference is related to the learning material itself.

When this is the case, it is necessary to increase the attention-provoking properties of the relevant stimuli.

For example, in teaching a child to say dee when he sees the letter *d,* care must be taken to reduce interference from the letter *b.* One way to do this is to call attention to the differences between the two letters at the outset of discrimination training by showing the loop of the *d* in red and by exaggerating the size of the loop. The size and color prompts can then be gradually eliminated as the child learns to make the appropriate response dee to *d.* In the technical language of programmed instruction, this technique is referred to as "vanishing" or "fading" of prompts.

Techniques of establishing stimulus control have played a large role in the development of educational technology. The need for special visual media such as motion pictures and television, and for special auditory media such as tape recordings, records, and the language laboratory systems is a function of the stimulus characteristics of the material to be learned.

The Question of Motivation

The *S-R* reinforcement model does not generate separate questions about the process of motivation, but questions about motivation are considered in dealing with reinforcement. A learner must be sufficiently motivated to work for reinforcers.

In this sense, motivation is virtually equated with deprivation in the case of positive reinforcement, or with the presentation of aversive events in the case of negative reinforcement. A poorly motivated learner is simply one for whom few if any reinforcers are effective; a highly motivated learner is one for whom a particular reinforcer or a variety of reinforcers is effective.

Another way to state this is: It is difficult to teach an unmotivated student because he is not responsive to reinforcement, while it is easy to teach a motivated student, because he is responsive to reinforcement.

The Model in Use

Consider the problem of teaching ninth-grade students the units of length in the metric system of measurement. The analysis of this problem is shown below in terms of answers to the questions generated by the *S-R* reinforcement model. These questions are summarized in Table 4-1 as questions of analysis and questions of implementation.

The analysis questions are dealt with first and then consideration is given to the implementation in terms of response, reinforcement, and stimulus factors.

Analysis: Responses

Responses to be learned. The responses to be learned include the following:

(a) Labeling responses. These include in terms of decimal equivalents the metric measures: millimeter (mm), centimeter (cm), decimeter (dm), meter (m), and kilometer (km), including the current spelling of the words and the correct usage of their abbreviations.

Table 4-1. Questions generated by the *S-R* reinforcement model
of teaching

RESPONSES

Analysis

1. What are the responses to be learned?
2. Are these novel or familiar to the learner?

5. What responses may compete?

Implementation

3. How is the learner to become familiar with the response?
4. How are the appropriate responses to be evoked?

6. How can response competition be reduced?

REINFORCEMENT

Analysis

1. What reinforcers are likely to be effective?

Implementation

2. How are these reinforcers to be applied?

STIMULI

Analysis

1. What are the relevant stimuli?

Implementation

2. How will they be associated with the appropriate responses?
3. How will interfering stimuli be controlled?

(b) Converting millimeters to centimeters, centimeters to decimeters, decimeters to meters, meters to kilometers; and converting centimeters to millimeters, decimeters to centimeters, and so forth; and adding metric units, for example 3 mm plus 19 cm plus 6.3 m.

(c) Measuring length using a ruler 30 cm long, marked off in cm and mm. The measures are to be expressed in the appropriate whole unit with fractional amounts expressed in decimal terms, for example, 4.5 cm, or 6.8 m, or 3 mm.

(d) Converting each of the metric measures into the English system and vice versa. For example, convert 32 m into feet and convert 17 inches into cm.

Familiarity. Some responses are unfamiliar. Words like decimeter (dm) and kilometer (km) may require familiarization training.

Sources of response competition. The responses, one thousand to the stimulus kilo and one thousandth to the stimulus milli will compete with each other.

Analysis: Reinforcement

The model does not identify reinforcers per se. It merely calls attention to the requirement that responses must be reinforced if they are to be strengthened. The implementation of reinforcement is handled by the model and is discussed below.

Analysis: Stimuli

The relevant stimuli include the following:

(a) The words themselves and their abbreviations. Centimeter is a response, but it is also a stimulus. For example, "How many centimeters are there in an inch?" is a stimulus, setting the occasion for the response, "2.54 cm."

(b) Fractions or decimals such as 5/10 cm or .1 m

(c) scale readings on a metric ruler, for example

(d) English measures such as inch, foot, yard, mile.

Implementation

(a) Labeling responses

Familiarization of responses. A safe assumption is that some, if not all, of the words are unfamiliar and require familiarization training, often referred to as response training. This training consists of exposing the learner to written material in which he sees and reads these words in a meaningful context. For example, the learner may be given the following paragraph with instructions to read it and to try to answer the question that follows it:

Bill carefully measured the table and found it 78 centimeters (cm) wide and 2.3 meters (m) long. His friend, John, lived 1 kilometer (km) away, and he did not wish to carry the table that distance only to find it would not fit through John's doorway. He telephoned John and was told the doorway measured 7.5 decimeters (dm) wide by 2,290 millimeters (mm) high.

Question: Would the table fit through John's doorway?

Hints: A decimeter (dm) is 10 centimeters (cm).

A meter (m) is 100 cm.

A millimeter (mm) is 1/1000 of a m.

Evoking the responses to be learned. The labelling responses may be initially evoked by means of prompts and then reinforced by arranging question-and-answer sequences using confirmation of correct responses (positive feedback) as the immediate reinforcer. For example, to teach the response *centimeter* the following item may be presented visually or auditorily:

A meter can be divided into 100 parts; each of these parts is called a *centi*meter. A cent is 1/100 of a dollar and a _____ meter is 1/100 of a meter.

In the above item the response "centi" is prompted by the emphasis on centimeter when the word is first presented, and by reference to cent. The reinforcing event is seeing or hearing the correct response and confirming that one's own response was correct.

Associating the relevant stimuli with the appropriate responses. To get the response *centimeter* to occur at a proper time in the proper context, it must be associated with relevant stimuli, for example, 1/100 of a meter or 10 millimeters, or 1 decimeter. The following item illustrates the procedure:

1/100 of a meter is a _____, and

1/100 of a dollar is a cent.

In the above item a prompt (cent) is still present to ensure the response centimeter in the presence of the stimulus 1/100 of a meter. When prompts are given, the correct response is easily forthcoming and consequently the confirmation of the correct response is less reinforcing than it would be for a more challenging question such as the following:

There are 100 _____ in a meter.

The abbreviation for centimeter can be taught using essentially the same type of approach: evoke it using prompts, reinforce it, associate it with the relevant stimuli and reinforce the association. The following items illustrate how this could be done:

(1) The abbreviation for centimeter involves the c for centi and the m for meter. Give the abbreviation for centimeter.

(2) 3/100 of a meter is equal to 3 _____ (use abbreviation).

The reader will recognize the above items as examples of one of the programmed instruction methods, a method derived from the *S-R* reinforcement model.

The same general approach described above may be used to elicit the responses *decimeter* and *kilometer* and to associate them with the relevant controlling stimuli. However, a special problem arises in the case of teaching millimeter because of response competition between the responses one thousand to the stimulus kilo and the response one thousand*th* to the stimulus milli.

This response competition may be reduced by exaggerating or dramatizing the differences between the two responses, between the stimuli and between the stimulus-response associations.

The responses can be differentiated best by initially requiring that they be made in decimal form, for example, 1000 and .001. The two stimulus-response associations can be differentiated by giving them certain distinguishing characteristics.

For example, since kilo refers to the large unit, it may be shown in capital letters, KILO; and milli, because it refers to the small unit, may be shown in small letters, milli. The size of the letters is a prompt, enabling the learner to recognize that one calls for a large number and the other for a small number.

The purpose of such an artifice is to maximize the probability the learner will not confuse the two associations and make the wrong response to either stimulus. According to the model, the learner learns what he does, and, if he makes errors, they will be learned and later have to be extinguished.

In teaching discrimination, it is useful to keep in mind the rule that learner errors are to be avoided. Where errors occur and are difficult to avoid, as might be the case in teaching the pronunciation of Saint-Cloud, steps must be taken to extinguish the competing responses.

(b) Converting metric units into other metric units and adding metric units

The responses of converting metric units into other metric units and adding metric units are essentially the same as those involved in identifying the decimal equivalents of the metric units.

Once these decimal equivalents are learned, they can be used to mediate in the chain of responses required to convert or add units.

A student can quickly learn that a dm consits of 10 cm after he has learned that 1 mm is .1 cm, or that 1 cm is .01 m and 1 mm is .001m. Of course, if the student cannot work with decimal numbers, he will not see the relationships. In this case, the teaching task would be a much larger one, beginning with instruction in fractions and decimals.

(c) Measuring Length

The responses of measuring length are to be associated with the stimuli of the scale readings on a metric ruler. It will be assumed that the students are familiar with English-unit rulers, so no familiarization training is required.

The task entails making measurements by reading them from a metric scale to the nearest whole unit. This is effectively done in two stages. In the first stage, the student merely measures a number of lines comparing his measurements with those that are provided for feedback. In the second stage, more interesting tasks are used, and consequently the reinforcing effects of confirming correct responses is stronger.

A sample task might be the following:

Line A is 4.6 cm long. Guess the length of line B and write it here

------------------------- .

Now measure line B to see how accurate your guess was.

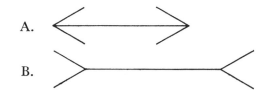

A.

B.

(d) Converting metric units into English units and English into metric

Learning to convert metric units into English units is a straight-forward association task. The metric units serve as stimuli and the English units as the responses. For example, the students are taught to give the response ".39 inches" to the stimulus, "How many inches are there in 1 cm?"

In this type of task, sequence can be important. The order in which the material is presented can be a source of interference, or, if properly used, it can be put to advantage.

In this conversion task, the optimal sequence would involve rank-ordering the responses from smallest to largest in the following manner: 1 cm = .39 inches, 1 m = 39.37 inches, and 1 km = .62 miles.

Learning the reverse conversion requires only one item: 1 inch = 2.54 cm.

There is nothing gained by requiring the student to memorize the metric equivalent for foot, yard, and mile.

Actually, this additional memorization would be disadvantageous, because the additional associations introduce a needless source of additional interference. The conversions for foot, yard, and mile are easily calculated once the student has learned the metric equivalent for an inch.

The Model and Retention and Transfer of Learning

The problems associated with teaching are interwoven with questions about the retention and transfer of learning. Any model that purports to deal with learning must, if it is to prove useful, deal also with the conditions that affect retention and transfer.

In terms of the *S-R* reinforcement model, questions about retention become questions about the conditions that control and maintain responses. Since responses are put under the control of particular stimuli and the occurrence of the responses in the presence of these stimuli depends on reinforcement, our attention is directed to stimulus factors and reinforcement factors. These factors lead to three general principles relating to methods of increasing retention.

(1) Retention can be increased by using intermittent schedules of reinforcement to maintain the responses once they are learned.

For example, a response that is reinforced on an average of 7 out of 10 times after it is learned persists for a longer period after reinforcement has been terminated, than one which has been continuously reinforced, that is, every 10 out of 10 times.

(2) Retention is increased by increasing the number and variety of stimuli associated with a particular response. This may be done by having the learner relate what he is learning to other stimuli as well as those he is now learning. This procedure may be described as giving the material meaning. It also helps to have the learner practice the responses in a variety of settings so that they do not become limited to a particular setting. The more settings a response is associated with, the greater the chance that the response can be evoked in any setting.

(3) Retention is helped by seeing to it that no new responses are associated with the relevant stimuli between the time of learning and the time of retention testing. If a given stimulus has been associated with a particular response and then another response is paired with

that stimulus, the chance of the first response occurring is reduced.

For example, if a student learning a list of state capitals has learned the response Columbus to the stimulus Ohio, and he later learns the response Cleveland to the same stimulus in a slightly different context, the two responses may compete when he is asked to name the capital city of Ohio. While one of the names will emerge, the probability of its being the correct one is reduced by the competition. The competition between the responses interferes with retention of the correct response.

The transfer of learning is critically influenced by the similarity between the learning task and the task to which transfer is being made. If task *A* is similar to task *B* in terms of the responses called for, then what is learned in *B* will transfer positively to *B*. The responses learned in *A* will assist in the performance or the learning of *B*.

For example, learning the metric units of length will provide positive transfer to learning weight and volume, because the prefix responses have the same meaning: milli is 1/1000 whether it precedes meter, gram, or liter.

If task *A* is similar to *B* in terms of the stimuli, but the responses in the two tasks are different, then *A* will negatively influence (interfere with) *B*. For example, learning the French words for the parts of the body will transfer negatively to a task which requires learning the Italian words for these same parts. The stimuli are the same, but many of the responses are different.

The Model and Technology

An analysis of a teaching problem in terms of the *S-R* reinforcement model does not lead directly to the use of specific instructional techniques, nor does such an analysis necessarily suggest devices or specialized training aids. Techniques, aids, and devices are developed in terms of answers to the questions raised by the language and mode of analysis of the model.

The model tells us to get the responses to occur. To do this effectively a device may be necessary. Devices are particularly useful in presenting prompts and in fading out prompts.

The model tells us to reinforce responses immediately and frequently. To do this we must have either a one-to-one teacher to student ratio or devise some techniques and/or devices. The reader will recognize the development of teaching machines and programmed instruction in these terms.

The model tells us to identify the relevant stimuli and to associate them with the appropriate responses. To do this, techniques of stimulus presentation are needed, and very often special devices, for example, films, television, recordings, mock-ups, and so forth play an important role.

5. Some Economic Models of Curriculum Structure

Ralph F. Goldman, William H. Weber,
and *Harold J. Noah*

Those interested in the economics of education have long concerned themselves with investigating the relationships which appear to exist between education and socioeconomic development. A number of studies have attempted to show the existence of a systematic relationship between school enrollment as a percentage of age group, or stock of educated manpower, and a nation's "stage of development." These studies search for systematic regularities across countries at a point in time and, in the case of individual countries, through time.[1] Most, if not all, such investigations suffer from their restricted formulation in terms of investment-in-human-capital models and their implicit assumption that, if economic and social development is to occur, educational patterns must be established which mirror those of developed Western nations. This approach, although capable of producing interesting results, fails to raise many more exciting questions which a somewhat broader application of economic model building can generate.[2]

The two fairly speculative models presented in this paper illustrate some less restrictive techniques of economic model building. The

Reprinted with the permission of *Teachers College Record* (73 [December 1971], 285-303) and the authors.

first model is the microeconomic type. It suggests that if a school district wishes to maximize student learning, there may exist an optimal teacher salary level it should pay, given the student ability to learn, the distribution of abilities in the population of teachers currently in the market, and certain other conditions of supply and demand. The second model is macrosocioeconomic, and suggests possible relationships among higher education curriculum, economic and technological change, and social change.

What immediately follows contains a broad overview of the problems which the individual school district faces in adjusting to changing social and economic conditions.

Economic Aspects of Public Schooling

The public school curriculum, viewed in its entirety, appears to the economist as a community-purchased and -distributed bundle of teacher-pupil interactions, carried out over a carefully defined period of time. Public provision to the school-age population of free access to these interactions is prescribed by custom, mandated by law, and justified by the contribution which pupil participation in these interactions is expected to make to the improvement of the milieu. The community provides the curriculum not as a final product, that is, not as an end in itself, but as an intermediate product, exposure to which is expected to produce within the pupil reactions commonly identified as knowledge, skills, and attitudes. These reactions are presumably transformed by the pupil, to a degree that varies with the individual, into that capacity for civilized thinking (and constructive action in accordance with that thinking) called education.

The community therefore does not provide education; it provides only the curriculum. Whether the pupil succeeds in transforming his exposure to the curriculum into the final good called education rests on other factors, such as general and school environment, family background, and the impact of these on the individual's genetic endowment. However, the pupil can gain access to the curriculum only upon condition of compulsory participation in, or at least exposure to, the institutionalizing process of schooling. The curriculum is imbedded in schooling and, therefore, for public purposes is inseparable from it. Hence, this paper speaks not of the "demand for education," or of the "demand for curriculum," but rather of the "demand for (public) schooling."

The interactions which comprise the curriculum are produced by combining in varying proportions the traditional economic inputs of land, labor, and capital. In the schooling context, these scarce resources include school buildings, materials, and supplies (both instructional and noninstructional); time of administrators and auxiliary personnel; time of teachers; and time of pupils.

The time of pupils is considered to have zero money value since, at least until the age of sixteen, the pupil is not regarded as sacrificing earnings in order to attend school. The time of teachers, however, is recognized as having considerable money value, as reflected in the fact that teachers' salaries absorb about 50 percent of the total U.S. expenditure on public elementary and secondary schooling.

However, a curriculum is essentially a structuring of the time of all participants, pupils as well as teachers. The cost of structuring time to produce Curriculum Pattern A is reckoned in terms of the educational benefits that might have been enjoyed by pupils if the time had instead been structured to produce an alternative, Curriculum Pattern B. The cost of A can also be reckoned in terms of the inputs unproductively expended by failing to adopt alternative B.

Thus the structuring of time by which a given curriculum pattern is produced implies an economic trade-off—that is, certain curriculum features thought to be desirable are obtained at the expense of the efficient use of certain inputs. However, the inputs presently under consideration are not among those included in the traditional list. Rather, they are the scarce human resource inputs which are always assumed to exist in sufficient quantity to guarantee the viability of each alternative curriculum pattern. However, these inputs are rarely included in analyses of the curriculum production function, even though they are at its very core. Despite the obvious difficulties of measurement, these inputs should at least be included as residuals, since not a single minute in the schooling process passes that does not somehow involve their expenditure.

These scarcer inputs are, on the teacher's side, the ability to teach and the desire to teach; and, on the pupil's side, the ability to learn and the desire to learn. The twin problems of pupil dropout and teacher turnover are only now focusing our attention on the urgent need for conserving, and possibly expanding, these very scarce human resource factors, which are coming to be recognized as inputs that are variable, both upward and downward, in the schooling process. Since economics concerns itself with the allocation of scarce resources of whatever form, these too deserve at least to be mentioned in any analysis of the demand for curriculum qua schooling, and to be given a priority rating on the list of topics for further research.

Analysis of the demand for schooling starts by considering the demand of individual private purchasers for that type of curriculum whose benefits would accrue primarily to them privately. In this private-consumer context, the demand for curriculum may be predicted from the traditional theory of consumer behavior. Thus in times of prosperity, as the relative price of education appears to decline, private consumers will demand longer periods of schooling. Even in times of general economic adversity, if consumers' information indicates that schooling is retaining or expanding its satisfaction-maximizing capacity, private consumers will demand more schooling, even if the price rises.

However, the demand for schooling by a community, which is required to distribute it to the public, functions somewhat differently. Whereas the demand of the individual private purchaser is motivated by voluntarism, the demand of the community, the collective purchaser, is motivated by statutory compulsion. Moreover, the community is placed in the position of sole purchaser of the principal purchasable input to the process—the supply of certified teachers. As long as school enrollment remains fairly stable, the community as sole purchaser of this input is in a favored position and encounters no problem in meeting the demand for curriculum.

As school enrollment rises, however, the community's usage of certified teachers expands, and the price of this input increases. The community, however, is prevented by law from reducing its production of the schooling service which makes use of this input. If the community's production of schooling continues to expand, as made inevitable by rising enrollments, the additional expense of hiring one more teacher reaches the level at which quantitative demand for curriculum can be met only by purchasing lower-priced, lower-quality input. The community thus produces an output in period 2 which, though quantitatively "correct" from the standpoint of number of classes covered, is likely to be qualitatively below that of period 1. It is, therefore, apparent that the community is not as free as the individual consumer to reduce its demand for quantity-of-schooling-service-produced in response to rises in input price.

Nor is the community free to continue indefinitely lowering the quality of input, particularly in the form of labor. Negative output effects will soon evoke objections from pupils and parents on grounds of deteriorating quality of service. Objections will come, interestingly enough, from both the poor and the middle class, but for different reasons. The poor see the curriculum as a means for redistributing community wealth through the promise of additional earning power for their children as well as through the value of the service provided; the middle class sees the curriculum as a means of maintaining their income lead and getting a proper return on their property tax. Political considerations will soon compel the community to substitute inputs of capital for the now excessively costly labor in an attempt to maintain quality as well as quantity of output. However, no relationship between resource input and curriculum output has yet been demonstrated. Hence the allocation pattern thus produced may be suboptimal, reminding us that the curriculum itself is often a suboptimal solution under a set of constraints which are not only economic but also social and political.

Generally, public schooling seems to be a "normal" good, with increase in money income leading to increase in consumption. Communities with higher per capita wealth commonly exhibit a willingness to purchase more units of curriculum for their schooling process than communities with lower per capita wealth. Even in communities with relatively low tax yields, however, external factors may increase the intensity of the local desire for schooling. Thus in the late 1950's, buying more units, and more expensive units, of curriculum became a way of demonstrating the community's patriotic determination to compete with the Soviets. Or, as an additional example, pressure in the job market may cause a rise in the demand for schooling. In response to a rapidly expanding labor force, as a result of demographic trends, employers set up increasingly stringent schooling requirements as bases for selecting applicants. These rising expectations of employers are given wide publicity and are soon matched by rising local demand for schooling. As a third example of external forces, changes in public taste can also cause a decline in the demand for specific types of schooling, such as instruction in foreign languages.

Prices of related commodities also condition the level of demand for schooling. The rising cost of other public services has generated increasing resistance to school budget proposals, in effect communicating local desire to reduce the quantity of schooling to be purchased by the community. Nevertheless, the public insists, too, that this reduction not take place at the expense of curriculum quality. Accordingly, some school boards take this as a mandate for exchanging a large number of lower-quality teachers for a smaller number of higher-quality teachers, coupling this teacher redeployment with such innovations as modular scheduling, team teaching, technological devices for instruction, a loosely structured school day, and relaxation of behavioral standards requiring many teachers and much teacher time for enforcement. Other school boards have interpreted community resistance to school budget proposals as a mandate to hire young, relatively inexperienced, and hence lower-salaried teachers as less expensive inputs. Veteran tenured teachers who become aware of this trend in their districts have adopted the rule of thumb that, when a salary of a tenured teacher reaches the level, under the automatic increment system, where it is equal to the salaries of two beginning teachers, the experienced teacher can expect to come under pressure to resign. The replacing of experienced by inexperienced teachers has brought in its wake a rising demand for instructional materials in "teacher-proof" packages guaranteed to place minimum demand on the skill and inventiveness of the replacement.

Can other commodities be substituted for the curriculum so that a rise in the price of schooling would lead to a positive change in the consumption of substitutes? The legitimate possibilities for substitution are presently limited because schooling in the traditional form is required by law. However, if public opinion can be conditioned to accept the relaxation of the compulsory aspect, many substitutes will become available and will enjoy increasing demand. The avalanche of publicity now accorded to "free schools," "alternative schools," and other informal schooling agencies may well be a step toward relaxation of the compulsory aspect, at least on a de facto, if not a de jure, basis. In the meantime public school authorities may be expected to move with increasing alacrity to expunge those institutional aspects of public schooling which encourage young people to seek alternative agencies of schooling outside the public jurisdiction. Indeed, if fear of political unrest and social dislocation were not looming in the background to dampen efforts at fundamental school reform, public education authorities might well be inclined to discontinue production of traditional schooling with all the dispatch with which industry closes down its production of manufactured goods that are no longer in demand due to the invention of acceptable substitutes available at lower prices.

The public, however, has not been conditioned to accept the rate of change in social arrangements, especially those sponsored by local authorities, that it has come to accept for technical innovation. Hence it is possible that social changes will occur only as technological innovations make them inevitable. Substitute commodities for the traditional schooling service can be expected to gain acceptance only where technological changes make relaxation of the compulsory aspect of public schooling seem reasonable.

A decline in demand for curriculum due to the availability of noncompulsory substitutes is a prospect for the long run. More immediate is the problem of the apparent declining demand for schooling on the part of its direct recipients, the pupils.

As reflected in classroom apathy and schoolwide unrest, the declining pupil demand for traditional schooling may well be the counterpart to the community's increased usage of lower-quality inputs, both instructional and physical, as substitutes for the more expensive inputs. Not infrequently the use of lower-quality inputs is justified on grounds that pupil performance does not warrant the use of costlier inputs. By this logic of self-fulfilling prophecy, community investment in schooling and pupil performance in the classroom must chase each other downward, presumably to the point at which the public recognizes that continued support of a nonfunctional "school" system is a misapplication of community resources. What is to be feared most, however, is not that a once-respected but now obsolete social form will disappear from the public scene but that, by the time society manages to overcome its social conservatism long enough to make the decision, it will have sustained irreparable damage to perhaps the scarcest of all human resources—pupils' ability and desire to learn, and teachers' ability and desire to teach.

Model I: Optimal Teacher Salary and the Production Function

As stated earlier, the economist looks upon the entire public school curriculum as a community-purchased and -distributed block of teacher-pupil interactions performed over a specific time period and expected to produce knowledge and attitude changes in the minds of the students.[3] The demands for teacher services and educational facilities derive from the community demand for the benefits which flow from living in an environment where some minimum level of educational attainment and set of attitudes can be presumed to be embodied in the individual members of the community. Thus the demand for free and required primary and secondary education is, at base, a demand for curriculum, where *curriculum* is broadly defined as teacher-pupil interactions so structured as to produce knowledge and attitude changes (socialization) in the minds of students.[4] In this sense, the curriculum may be regarded as the production process whereby inputs are converted into desired outputs, and determination of the cost of an increment of desired output requires an understanding of the technical relationships which exist between productive inputs and desired (and, perhaps, undesired) outputs. This "technical relationship" economists refer to as the production function.

Economists working in the economics of education have given a great deal of attention to the problem of calculating the returns, both direct (as experienced by the educated individual) and indirect (as experienced collectively by the community), generated by various levels and distributions of educational investment (investment in human capital). However, virtually no attention has been directed to the "education production function" at the level of the individual firm (school). The common approach is to consider the problem from the aggregate standpoint: What are the costs, as "objectively estimated," in terms of resources absorbed, including student income foregone, and what are the direct returns in terms of income differentials attributable to a given level of educational attainment, as well as the indirect returns in terms of increased productivity for others, rate of economic development, improvement of the milieu, and so on? Comparison of investment costs with the estimated money value of the direct and indirect returns yields a rate of return which can be compared with the return being earned on other kinds of investments. If the rate of return to educational investment exceeds that earned in noneducational investment, it can then be concluded that community welfare (under the assumption that a greater dollar value of GNP is always "better") would be improved through a reallocation of the resources which the community has somehow determined to allocate to investment rather than to present consumption. Reallocation would continue until the rate of return on all investments is brought into equality. The investment pattern which equalizes marginal returns from all investments is an efficient pattern simply because it cannot be improved upon; however, this, as we hope to demonstrate, is an incomplete analysis of the problem.

Neoclassical microeconomic theory finds investment to be efficient when incremental increases in investment in all areas yield identical returns; however, underlying this particular efficiency criterion are a number of assumptions, including the assumption of efficiency in production. The theoretical requirements for efficient industrial production have long been known, and this knowledge rests upon a large literature dealing with the characteristics of the industrial firm's production function. Although practical investigation of production functions in industry is logically the business of engineers, economists have never shown any disciplinary reserve about working in the theoretical aspects of input-output relations and, in fact, have made substantial contributions to this field. The results obtained from analyses of production functions in industry have not been used to help understand input-output relations in education. On the contrary, economists have been quite reluctant to engage in theoretical work on the school's production function. The result has been a "black box" approach to the education firm.[5] This is an unfortunate state of affairs, for a microeconomic analysis of the educational industry is both important and possible. The following is offered in the belief that such an analysis cannot be achieved in the absence of some theoretical generalizations concerning the nature of the educational firm's production function.

Figure 5-1A. shows the supply and demand conditions facing a given educational firm, a school district. Given such matters as plant and equipment, past school performance, local economic conditions, state and federal aid, projected enrollment, and teacher turnover, there will be a demand schedule in the local market, D_{LM}, for additional and replacement teachers.[6] Given the existing "image" of the school district in the minds of prospective teachers, the district's recruitment effort, the output of teachers from regional colleges and universities, and the recruiting efforts and images of competing school districts, there is an effective supply schedule of teachers to the local market, S_{LM}, such that at any given wage (or salary) a determinate number of teachers would offer themselves for employ-

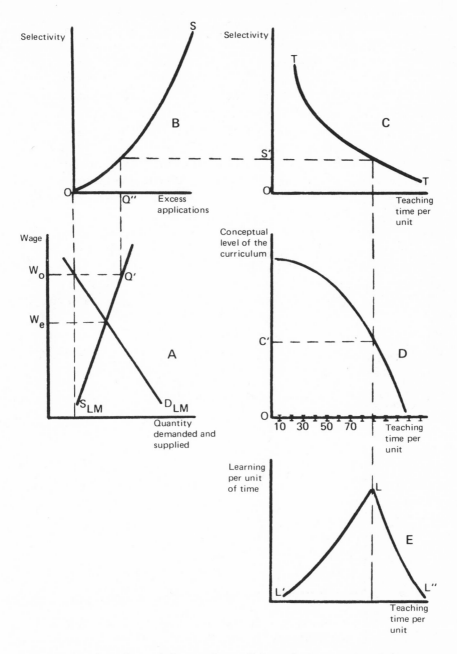

Figure 5-1. Supply and demand conditions facing a school district

ment. Under the temporary assumption that the wage paid to new teachers will not affect the wages of presently employed staff, W_e, is simply a price paid to recruit new teachers. It is not the system-determined wage because D_{LM} is not derived through marginal productivity analysis; that is, there is no school district analogue to marginal revenue product. Nor is there, for the moment, a school district analogue to the monopsonist's marginal supply price of labor.[7]

It is important to note at this point that the effective supply of teachers at any wage, S_{LM}, is not homogeneous as to quality, an index of which could be constructed from information concerning the selectivity of the college attended by the teacher, the teacher's academic record, and the information contained in the teacher's letters of recommendation.[8] Figure 5-2 illustrates a hypothetical frequency distribution by quality level of teachers currently in the market. Some of the more important factors affecting the area of the frequency distribution are the general market for teachers, the regional capacity for producing teachers, and the level of college enrollment. Some of the more important factors influencing the shape of the frequency distribution are the quality of teacher education programs in regional colleges, state certification requirements, and the status system "controlling" recruitment to public school teaching.[9]

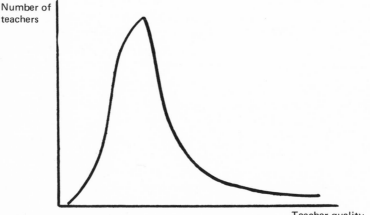

Figure 5-2. Hypothetical frequency distribution of teachers by quality level

It may be supposed, for example, that the area under the curve might be reduced and the skewness also reduced by changes in state certification requirements which de-emphasized methods courses and emphasized preparation in the subject to be taught.

As the wage level is increased, it is hypothesized that the number of applications from higher-quality teachers also increases, permitting, under conditions of excess applications, a higher average quality of teacher in the group employed. Given the beliefs of the school board concerning desirable teacher-student ratios and the conditions of supply and demand as indicated in Figure 5-1A, the board determines to hire a teacher group, size OH, of fairly high quality. To this end, it offers a wage of W_o, and receives applications in $W_o Q'$ quantity, or, looking at Figure 5-1B, it receives OQ'' number of excess applications. The selectivity function, OS, Figure 1B, is determined by the influence of W_o on the number of applications received from the high quality end of the teacher distribution, Figure 5-2. The selectivity function will shift up and become steeper the greater the area of the frequency distribution to the right of the modal class.

With OQ'' excess applications, a selectivity level of OS', Figure 5-1C, is attained. It is hypothesized that the higher the average teacher quality, the lower the time required to teach a given class of students a given "unit" of knowledge. The relationship between selectivity-level and teaching time/unit of knowledge is shown in Figure 5-1C as Curve TT. It is hypothesized that increases in the selectivity level yield diminishing marginal returns in terms of reductions in teaching time/unit.[10] Nevertheless, it is predicted that teaching time/unit will fall absolutely as a function of increases in teacher quality.

Teaching time/unit falls, it is hypothesized, because the higher-quality teacher has both the ability and the inclination to present the unit at a higher level of conceptualization, emphasizing the operation of general principles and the broader implications of the "information" contained in the unit, rather than the "facts" approach characteristic of teaching at lower levels of conceptualization (Figure 5-1D). It is also hypothesized that students respond positively, up to some point, to increases in the pace at which knowledge is presented; however, pace cannot be effectively increased, except when the reference pace has been quite low, without a concomitant increase in the level of conceptualization.[11] Figure 5-1E indicates the hypothesized "learning effect" of a more rapid delivery of the knowledge contained in the unit.

As indicated in Figure 5-1E, for any group of students, given their abilities, school experience, socioeconomic environment, and school facilities, there is some optimal teaching time/unit, which implies some optimal conceptual level of the curriculum, such as OC', Figure 5-1D. Figure 5-1C indicates that level of selectivity consistent with these optima, and Figure 5-1A indicates the level of wage, given conditions of supply and demand, which will lead to the achievement of the postulated optima.

As we have developed the educational production function, it is a relationship between the quality of teacher input and output in terms of increased learning/unit of time. Given S_{LM} and D_{LM}, teacher quality is seen as functionally related to the wage level. The $L'L_o$ portion of the learning curve indicates that, up to some critical point, the rate of increase in learning/unit of time rises as teaching time/unit falls; however, Curve TT indicates that the rate of decrease in teaching time/unit falls as teacher quality increases. Although the interaction of these two relationships would differ from school to school and, for any one school, from one time period to the next, we will assume that for the "representative" school (the analogue to Marshall's "representative" firm)[12] there is a period of increasing returns to unit increases in teacher quality followed by a period of decreasing returns, as illustrated in Figure 5-3.

Now, assuming that the quantity of teachers demanded responds very inelastically to increases in the offered wage, the marginal cost of generating an increase in learning/unit of time can be approximated by multiplying the increase in offered wage necessary to generate the quality increase in learning/unit of time by the number of teachers to be employed. The cost so calculated is marginal cost per unit increase in learning/unit of time. From this information plus information concerning fixed costs, the total cost curve for the educational firm can be generated. Since the total revenue of a school varies with enrollment and not with quality of output, the school will operate at that level of learning/unit of time determined by the intersection of the horizontal total revenue curve and the rising total cost curve, that is, at the break-even point, as illustrated in Figure 5-4.

Total Cost is defined as the sum of fixed plus variable costs.

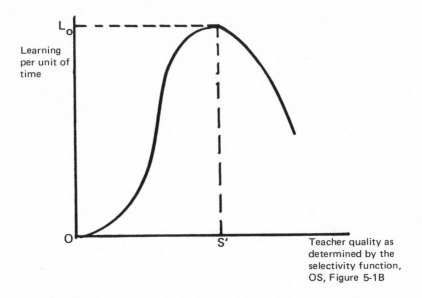

Figure 5-3. Relation between learning/unit of time
and teacher quality

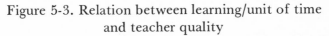
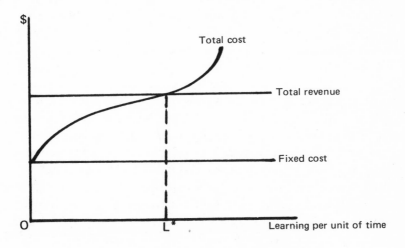

Figure 5-4. Relation between total revenue
and total cost in a school

Variable cost, in our case, is the sum of the marginal costs incurred in increasing the level of learning/unit of time by one unit. Assuming that marginal product, measured in terms of the increase in learning/ unit of time per incremental increase in teacher quality, increases at a rate which exceeds the rate at which wages must be increased to generate the unit increase in teacher quality, marginal costs will be falling. This stage is likely to be followed by a stage of decreasing returns and increasing marginal costs. Such relationships will generate a total cost curve such as that illustrated in Figure 5-4. Although L_o is the maximum possible level of learning/unit of time (as in Figures 5-1E and 3), the actual level of learning/unit of time will be found to be L^*, Figure 5-4. This is the level imposed by the break-even requirement, assuming that the break-even point occurs below the maximum level, at a level of selectivity below S' and in the region of positive but diminishing marginal returns.

Given L^*, we will also know the conceptual level of the curriculum which the interaction of all these forces calls into being. Assuming that the school superintendent has no control over the wage he can offer, and very limited control over who stays and who leaves his teaching staff, the conceptual level of his system's curriculum is determined by the system's passive adjustment to changes in variables over which little or no policy control can be exercised. To the degree that control is possible, it would appear that the only strategy really open to the superintendent is active recruitment of high-quality teachers when openings in his system occur.

To the extent that curriculum reformers have directed their efforts to surface changes in the curriculum complex, to the development of new texts and supplementary materials, they have not gone to the heart of curriculum improvement. Such reforms work only a cosmetic change, while fundamental change must depend upon changes in the socioeconomic mechanisms that control recruitment to primary and secondary teaching. In the final analysis, what we imply through our emphasis on the conceptual level of the curriculum is that, within limits, it does not matter what subjects are taught; what matters is that what is taught be taught at the highest level of conceptualization consistent with student ability to comprehend.[13]

Model II: Technological Change, Social Change, and the Higher Education Curriculum

Beginning with Plato's *Republic,* continuing with Adam Smith's *Wealth of Nations* and on to the present, social theorists, and economists in particular, have been concerned with the relationship between education and economic-and-social development and change. There are a number of modern studies which have attempted to establish a relationship between the curricular pattern of a nation and that nation's "stage-of-development." Studies of this type often attempt to establish the existence of a systematic relationship between school and college enrollment as a percentage of age-group and curricular content and the resulting stage of development by examining a range of countries at a point in time and/or several countries over time. The models used are, by and large, ones which see causality as running first from education to development, and then back again through demand analysis from development to education through the effect of higher incomes on the demand for education. A rapid rate of economic development is assumed to raise the return to education as well as to increase the demand for education (as a capital good and as a consumer durable) often more than proportionately to the increase in incomes. Thus, education makes development possible, and economic development raises the demand for higher education as both an investment in human capital and as a source of present and future consumption benefits.[14]

During the early phases of development, it may be quite appropriate to operate with a model in which economic factors largely explain the growth and curricular composition of higher education; however, we will argue that, at some point in a society's socioeconomic development, it is necessary to base models on a theoretical structure which makes some direct provision for the impact of the broader societal forces on the course of higher education and the higher education curriculum. Assuming that the developed quasi-market nations of the Western community have reached the point at which the broader social forces are beginning to swamp the narrower economic forces, we need to begin some disciplined speculation on the possible interconnections between education, economy, and society.

Economists are quite familiar with the heuristic usefulness of the assumption that in any system or subsystem there exists a tendency to equilibrium. The assumption serves the economists in much the same way that functional prerequisites serve the sociologists; that is, it is a conceptual device which performs a directing and ordering service. Although many types of equilibrium states are recognized by the economic model builder, he will usually organize his first approximations on the assumption that there exists a systematic interrelationship between the variables such that there is a tendency to equilibrium. In the model developed here, it is this assumption which "determined" the particular set of functional relationships connecting higher education curriculum with technological and social change which we show diagrammatically in Figure 5-5.

The assumptions of the model shown in Figure 5-5 are as follows:

1. In advanced Western countries the composition of the higher education curriculum (defined as the division of offerings between subjects of a highly specialized nature and offerings of a general-integrative nature) is related to the rates of technological and social change.[15]

2. There exists a specifiable relationship between the percentage of offerings of a specialized nature and the supportable rate of technological change.[16]

3. Given the determinant rate of technological change, there is a rate of specialization (division of labor) and organizational differentiation which, in turn, results in the creation of new and the reordering of existing social positions (or statuses) such that a systematic alteration of moral, cognitive, and aesthetic norms occurs; that is, technological change induces social change, and a particular rate of technological change induces a particular rate of social change.[17]

4. If social order is to be maintained, a given rate of social change requires some minimum consideration of the unanticipated consequences arising out of that change; that is, a given rate of social change creates a social need for research in and the teaching of general-integrative (or interdisciplinary) studies.

5. There is a tendency for higher education to expand through increasing specialization and subdivision of knowledge and, hence, of subject offering.[18]

6. There is, on the other hand, a tendency for the higher education curriculum to respond to societal pressures for general-integrative studies, such as ecology or interdisciplinary social science.

Figure 5-5A shows along the 45 degree line all possible combinations of percentages of general and specialized studies in the higher education curriculum. Figure 5-5B indicates the general form of the

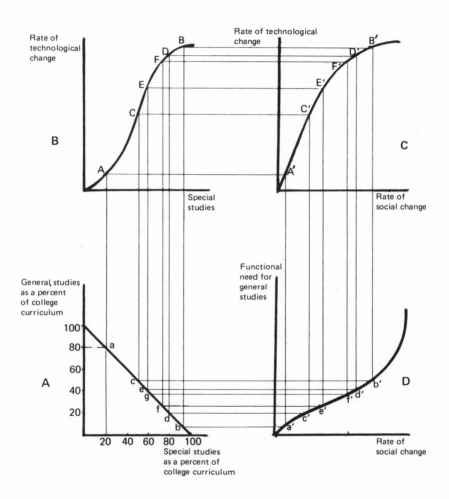

Figure 5-5. Functional relationships connecting
higher education curriculum with technological and social change

functional relationship assumed to exist between the percentage of specialized studies and the rate of technological change, *ceteris paribus.* Figure 5-5C shows the assumed relationship between the rate of technological change and the induced rate of social change, *ceteris paribus.* Figure 5-5D indicates the general nature of the relationship presumed to exist between the rate of social change and the societal need for general-integrative studies if social order is to be maintained at a given rate of social change.

Returning to Figure 5-5B, it is assumed that, other things being equal, such as enrollment in higher education, the resources devoted to higher education, and the present state of the economy, increases in the percentage of the higher education curriculum (HEC) devoted to special studies at first induce increasing rates of technological change, but as the specialized emphasis continues to increase, the rate of induced change levels off. This particular specification of the relationship would seem "reasonable," and, as its particular characteristics are not critical to the argument, a justification of this assumption need not be undertaken. That is, our results do not critically depend upon the shape of the technology function in Figure 5-5B.

In Figure 5-5C we indicate that higher rates of technological change induce increasing rates of social change. The reasoning behind this assumption is too complex to be elaborated here, but we would hold that our assumption is consistent with Talcott Parsons' analysis of this identical problem in Chapter XI, "The Processes of Change of Social Systems," of *The Social System.*

The particular relationship between the rate of social change and the "need" for general-integrative studies is built upon a host of assumptions concerning the operation and adequacy of the society's socialization mechanisms and the mechanisms of social control. As indicated in Figure 5-5D, the marginal increase in the functional need for general studies is presumed to be fairly constant over a rather extended range of variations in the rate of social change. For our model to operate, it is only necessary to make the rather weak assumption that the need for general studies does not decrease with an increasing rate of social change. If the need function has either a constant or an increasing slope, the dynamic aspects of the posited system remain unchanged.

We have developed a dynamic equilibrium type model.[20] It is dynamic because the path to equilibrium is, to some degree, specified, and it is of the equilibrium (or stable equilibrium) type because any exogenous force which displaces the system from equilibrium will set in motion forces which will return it to equilibrium, if at a different point. The model posits that, given the factors which determine the exact shape and position of the functions specified in Figures 5-5B through 5-5D, there is a combination of HEC composition, rate of technological change, and rate of social change such that further system-induced changes in these variables will not take place.

If, for purposes of discussion, we assume instantaneous adjustment of all variables (when they are viewed as dependent variables) to the values called for by the value of their determining variables, we can trace the dynamic adjustment path illustrated in Figure 5-5.

Beginning with Figure 5-5A, we assume an HEC composition where 80 percent of the studies are general and 20 percent are specific, as indicated by point *a.* This combination induces a rate of technological change (RTC) of *A*; and *A* induces a rate of social change (RSC) of *A'*; and *A'* induces a need for general studies (NGS) of *a'*; and *a'* calls into being, following the tendency of higher education to be, so to speak, "as specialized as socially permissible," a new HEC composition, *b.* The process continues for a number of rounds until the equilibrium combination is determined.

Inasmuch as social systems do not adjust rapidly to changes in societal variables, the path we have just described would never be experienced. We simply do not observe the radical shifts in fundamental societal variables suggested by the path just described. Using a period analysis approach to the adjustments in this model, we again begin at point *a,* Figure 5-5A. Given composition *"a,"* the system of higher education is free to follow its tendency to expand through increasing specialization; that is, during the first period, point *a* is consistent with unconstrained movement from point *a* toward point *c,* Figure 5-5A. In the second period, the HEC composition is at point *c,* with functional need at point *d,* and the higher education system is still free to continue its growth, paralleling the general growth of the population and economy, through specialization and offering an increased percentage of specialized courses. In the third period, the higher education curriculum has reached point *e* and functional needs are calling for a minimum indicated by point *f.* Given the direction of movement in higher education, it may be expected that during the fourth period the system will "overshoot" the equilibrium combination and that a number of periods will be required for the system to settle down to its equilibrium point; however, the system operates to progressively dampen any oscillation about equilibrium. Looking at United States higher education, it would appear that a system of this type has been in operation for some fifty years and that we are now at point d while the RSC stands at B', Figure 5-5C, and Functional Need is calling for HEC combination point c. This mismatch between our actual curriculum composition and the needed curriculum composition is the result of an "overshoot" of the equilibrium combination and the tardy response of higher education to societal forces calling for an increase in the percentage of general-integrative studies and research.

Notes

1. Perhaps the best known of such studies is by F. Harbison and C. A. Myers, *Education, Manpower and Economic Growth* (New York: McGraw-Hill, 1964). The UNESCO publication, *Readings in the Economics of Education,* (Paris: UNESCO, 1968), reprints a number of articles connecting economic growth with education. Those interested in a sociological approach to the problem of education and socioeconomic development are strongly directed to Joseph Ben-David's OECD Monograph, *Fundamental Research and the Universities: Some Comments on International Differences.* (Paris: Organization for Economic Cooperation and Development, 1968).

2. Although many studies make use of C.E.S. production functions, one of the more interesting is by Marcelo Selowsky, "On the Measurement of Education's Contribution to Growth," *The Quarterly Journal of Economics* 83 (August 1968), 449-63. In this article international comparisons are drawn between Chile, Mexico, and India.

3. For a full discussion of what an economist means by "the production of knowledge," see especially Fritz Machlup, *The Production and Distribution of Knowledge in the United States* (Princeton, New Jersey: Princeton University Press, 1962), ch. 2.

4. A very interesting discussion of community demand for education is contained in Mark V. Pauly, "Mixed Public and Private Financing of Education," *American Economic Review* 57 (March 1967), 120-30. The literature on attitude change via a process of socialization is quite large. The following are representative sources of research: J. S. Coleman, *Education and Political Development* (Princeton, New Jersey: Princeton University Press, 1965); A. H. Halsen, Jean Floud, and C. Arnold Anderson (eds.), *Education, Economy, and Society* (New York: Free Press, 1961); C. H. Stember, *Education and Attitude Change,* (New York: Institute of Human Relations Press, 1961); and "Socialization and Schools," *Harvard Educational Review,* Reprint Series No. 1, 1968.

5. Two representative "black box" approaches are: Jesse Burkhead, *Input*

and Output in Large-City High Schools (Syracuse, New York: Syracuse University Press, 1967) and J. A. Kershaw and R. N. McKean, *Systems Analysis and Education*, RAND Corporation Monograph, Memorandum RM-2473-FF, October 1959. Another, if quite different, approach to efficiency in public education is found in Andre Daniere, *Higher Education in the American Economy* (New York: Random House, 1964), ch. 12.

6. Two basic theoretical discussions of the derivation of the demand curve for a factor of production are contained in J. R. Hicks, *Value and Capital* (New York: Oxford University Press, 1939), particularly chapter 7 and the Mathematical Appendix to chapter 7; and in Paul Samuelson, *Foundations of Economic Analysis*, (Cambridge, Mass.: Harvard University Press, 1947). A particularly helpful discussion of the issues raised by Hicks and Samuelson is contained in R. R. Russell, "A Graphical Proof of the Impossibility of a Positively Inclined Demand Curve for a Factor of Production," *American Economic Review* 54 (September 1964), 726-32.

7. A good discussion of these matters is contained in most price theory (or microeconomics) texts; however, one of the clearest discussions is in George Malanos, *Intermediate Economic Theory* (Philadelphia: Lippincott, 1962), ch. 18.

8. Concerning the relationship between teacher and student performance, a relationship about which we will have more to say later, the Corazzini study, *Higher Education in the Boston Metropolitan Area*, Vol. VI of the Board of Higher Education Series (Boston: the Board, 1969), notes that: "Teacher qualifications, as expressed by the highest level of teachers' educational attainment, proved not only to be a significant influence on measured student aptitude, but also one to which improvement in pupil performance was relatively responsive" (p. 95). They also note that: "Schools that tend to spend the most also tend to employ the younger, less costly teachers; an interesting trade-off in the expenditure of school dollars" (p. 23).

9. There has been a great deal of research done on the quality of teacher education programs and on the recruitment of undergraduates of teacher-training programs and undergraduates in other programs according to a number of factors, such as intellectual interest, motivation, and applied interests. See George C. Stern, "Student Ecology and the College Environment," *Research in Higher Education* (New York: College Entrance Examination Board, 1965), 35-52.

10. The determination of teaching time/unit could be undertaken in the following way: Teachers of a given quality are asked to prepare an academic unit that will require two class meetings of instruction. The bench mark unit, assuming it to be validated through the instruction of several matched classes of students (validated in the sense that it actually does take two class meetings of instruction when taught by teachers of a given quality), is given to a group of teachers of a higher quality, and they are asked to teach it with a minimum of modification to a group of students matched with those who participated in the establishment of the bench mark. It would be critical to the results of the experiment that the high-quality teachers not know that there was anything special about this assignment. It could be a part of a series of experiments.

11. Although a great deal could be written concerning the particulars of the published research dealing with the hypotheses formulated in this paragraph, we will have to limit our "discussion" to the citation of works which we see as supporting our hypotheses. As we read Piaget in *The Moral Judgment of the Child* and in *The Early Growth of Logic in the Child,* particularly as these works are seen through the work of O. J. Harvey, D. E. Hunt, and Harold M. Schroder, *Conceptual Systems and Personality Organization* (New York: John Wiley, 1961), we feel some confidence in the "reasonableness" of our formulation. As to what it is that we refer to when we speak of "the conceptual level of the curriculum," the following statement from Harvey *et al.* is offered: "We assume that an individual interacts with his environment by breaking it down and organizing it into meaningful patterns congruent with his own needs [which the teacher is acting to shape] and psychological makeup. As a result of this interchange, perceptual and behavioral constancies develop, which stem from the individual's standardized evaluative predilections toward differential aspects of his external world. We will refer to such evaluative tendencies as concepts. In serving as modes of relatedness or connecting ties between the individual and his environment, concepts thus provide the basis for understanding the joint effect of situational and dispositional factors." We argue that the curriculum of one school may quite usefully be distinguished from that of another based on the curriculum's efficiency in aiding the child to develop these subject-object ties, which we refer to as "the conceptual level of the curriculum."

12. Alfred Marshall, *Principles of Economics,* 8th ed. (New York: Macmillan, 1920), ch. 13.

13. In the matter of how a unit of secondary education may be organized to produce a curriculum having a high level of conceptualization, see William H. Weber, *The Centre Program for Project Opportunity,* report to the Ford Foundation published through the ERIC System of the U.S. Office of Education, Education Resources Information Center Document Number ED 024739, abstracted in *Research and Education* 4 (April 1969), 114.

14. The most extensive study of this type which deals with developed nations is Edward E. Denison, *Why Growth Rates Differ: Postwar Experience in Nine Western Countries* (Washington, D.C.: Brookings Institution, 1967), particularly ch. 8.

15. Concerning the notion of technological change and the measurement of such change, see Edwin Mansfield, *The Economics of Technological Change* (New York: W. W. Norton, 1968), particularly ch. 2.

16. There is much in the Machlup study, *op. cit.,* which supports this contention, although Machlup shows that, in the *original* development of new technical knowledge, higher education plans only a small role.

17. See, in particular, Talcott Parsons, *The Social System* (New York: Free Press, 1951), ch. 11. On a more philosophical plane, the (uncertain) relationship between man, science, and society as discussed by Floyd Matson, *The Broken Image* (New York: Anchor Books, 1966). In Matson we see "technological change in the broader context of "applied social science," an application which depends to a great extent on the spread of this knowledge through higher education.

18. For an account of how Harvard broadened its subject offerings while expanding in size, see Seymour E. Harris, *The Economics of Harvard* (New York: McGraw-Hill, 1970). If we take the appointment of (full) professors and associate professors as an index of the establishment of new teaching and research areas, it is interesting to note the increases in the percentage of professors and associate professors to total faculty at Harvard. These percentages have fluctuated widely over the years, but during the expansionary period from 1940 to 1960, the percentage of expanding faculty at these high ranks increased from 45 percent to 64 percent, indicating the establishment of many new teaching and research specializations (see Table 10-3, p. 128.)

19. The response of engineering departments to the present circumstances, that is, a reduced interest in traditional engineering programs and a reduced market for the graduates of these programs, is interesting to note. For a report of the efforts of one "engineering" college, see the *Lafayette Alumnus* (January 1971), particularly the articles "Enrollment Slump Hits Engineering" and "Arts and the Engineer."

20. The best short discussion of what economists mean when they talk about dynamic systems is contained in Fritz Machlup, "Statics and Dynamics: Kaleidoscopic Words," *Southern Economic Journal* 26 (October 1959), reprinted in *Essays in Economic Semantics* (New York: W. W. Norton, 1963). The "classic" book on the subject of dynamic models is William Baumol, *Economic Dynamics*, 2nd ed. (New York: Macmillan, 1959).

Selected References for Curriculum as Technology

Drumheller, Sidney J. "Curriculum Making as a Game-Designing Task," *Educational Technology* 12 (May 1972), 13-17.

Helvey, T. C. "Cybernetic Pedagogy," *Educational Technology* 9 (September 1969), 17-22.

Manning, William P. "Cost Analysis and Curriculum Decisions," *Educational Leadership* 27 (November 1969), 179-83.

Merrill, M. David. "Components of a Cybernetic Instructional System," *Educational Technology* 8 (April 1968), 5-10.

Rath, Gustave J. "Human Factors Engineering of Educational Systems," *Educational Technology* 8 (September 1968), 15-16.

Raulerson, J. D., Jr. "The Human as Information Processor: A Guide for Instructional Design," *Educational Technology* 11 (December 1971), 12-15.

Walsh, James A., Jr. "Some Psychological Bases for Educational Technology," *Educational Technology* 10 (January 1970), 17-18.

Part Three
Self-Actualization, or
Curriculum as Consummatory Experience

This orientation to curricular thought refers to the goals espoused by its adherents. Schooling is to become a means of personal fulfillment, to provide a context in which individuals discover and develop their unique identities. Curriculum, in this view, is a pervasive and enriching experience with implications for many dimensions of personal development. "Curriculum as consummatory experience" is a broader and more demanding conception of schooling than either the cognitive processes or the curricular technology approach. Joseph Junnell's article (Chapter 6) provides an introduction to this orientation by questioning the traditional cognitive development commitments of education. Junnell suggests that curricula which neglect the nonrational aspects of personal growth are both inadequate and harmful. Philip Phenix' article (Chapter 7) is a particularly forceful example of the kinds of concerns, rationales, and goals demanded by a conception of curriculum which is permitted to expand beyond the cognitive development functions traditionally assigned to it. Phenix' conception of curriculum reflects a redefinition of the whole basis of education.

6. Is Rational Man Our First Priority?

Joseph S. Junell

In a provocative essay review of Arthur Schlesinger's book, *The Crisis of Confidence: Ideas, Power, and Violence in America,*[1] John Bunzel, newly appointed president of San Jose State College, raises a question to which every deeply concerned educator must ultimately turn his attention: To what part of man does public education owe its first obligation? Is it to his intellectual-academic world, or his emotional-social one? Which is most likely to insure him a measure of happiness and a reasonable chance for survival?

Mr. Bunzel's position on this matter is, of course, widespread among scholars throughout America. For both Bunzel and Schlesinger, the art of reflection is the only antidote to the insanity that daily encroaches upon our democratic way of life. Like Schlesinger, Bunzel "gives no quarter to those who would reject the process of reason" for the "simple ladling out of moral judgments."[2] He quotes the professor who insists that a "spectrum of opinion and action is indispensable if reason is to civilize power" and abjures within youth the "change in life-style which locates its center in a bewildering grab bag of sources that includes hallucinatory drugs and Eastern mystics,

Reprinted from *Phi Delta Kappan* 52 (November 1970), 147-51, with permission of the author and Phi Delta Kappa.

encounter groups and communal pads—in short, in the senses and emotions." Along with Schlesinger, his concern "is not simply the impulse to irrationalism which is evident everywhere, but the abandonment of rationality as a way to help set things right. . . . A liberal," he goes on to say, "does not deny or minimize the destructive tendencies that are a part of man's irrational component; rather, he reasserts the conviction that irrational motivations can best be treated at the conscious level, where they can be exposed to reason."[3]

Certainly there is much in Mr. Bunzel's words that compels admiration and a high level of agreement. There is also a certain naïveté to which historians are particularly prone. This naïveté is reflected in the belief that "reason" truly civilizes power, that "irrational motivations" are best corrected by exposing them to reason, or that "man's irrational component" is primarily destructive in nature. It is especially evident in the implication that the reasoning process can be trained to function without the influence of the senses and emotions.

Such indomitable faith in the powers of the mind to solve any or all problems can only be explained within the context of history. Its roots, as we know, are found in the age of rationalism, created by the extraordinary impact of ideas of such men as Copernicus, Kepler, Galileo, Newton, and Descartes. It was a world in which reason for the first time tried to provide "rational" controls for individual and social life, and in general to discard or minimize notions which were merely venerable, traditional, unproved, or irrational. To a large extent Montaigne abandoned his quest for absolute truth and advanced instead the virtues of doubt and tolerance. Bacon set his seal on inductive reasoning, and Descartes devoted himself to the task of reshaping philosophy into a pattern consistent with the new science. Among the learned it was a period of much optimism and hope, with a strong belief in rationality striking the central chord.

The movement did not progress without periods of strong reaction, of which the anti-intellectualism of Rousseau and Bergson are cases in point. Rousseau's concept of the noble savage, for example, is strongly reminiscent of much that is taking place among today's youth, as is also his rejection of reason in favor of conscience and feeling as the only true guides to correct social and moral behavior. Bergson's extravagances regarding the superiority of instinct and intuition over intellect are only slightly less well known. Thus the ideals recommended to us for the proper humanizing of man have tended to point sharply toward one extreme or the other. Each ideal has been founded on the concept of man's unlimited potential to achieve whatever he wants to achieve.

For the education of real children, however, the truth seems to lie somewhere in between, somewhere within an area which must take into account the unabashed acceptance of man's natural limitations. For instance, John Bowlby, in his *Maternal Care and Mental Health,* regards as one of the important psychiatric discoveries in the past half-century the lifelong influence of attitudes internalized during childhood. Although his pronouncement is based on studies conducted with emotionally deprived infants and children, it is forcibly brought home to us that the principles are the same for everyone; a gradual accumulation of preferences, compulsions, and rejections eventually forms our life-style. As the first evidences of organized behavior, they precede the development of rational thought. Whether they are healthy or diseased is of no immediate concern; what does concern us is that, good or bad, they cast over our lives an invisible screen of primary dispositions and tendencies to behavior through which each of our thoughts is sifted, and by which the very quality of our thinking is in large part determined.[4]

Evidence of man's emotionally dominated rational processes has been even further advanced in the past decade by the work of ethnologists such as Desmond Morris,[5] Konrad Lorenz,[6] and Robert Ardrey.[7] According to Morris, for instance, man emerged from the jungle onto the plains, a hunter, as aggressive and predatory as any animal on the scene. And so he remains, genetically unchanged, to this day. While he preens himself on the technical know-how of a vastly superior mentality, it is the emotions surrounding the territorial imperative and the development of sexual equipment, unique within the primate kingdom, which continue to hold him in thrall and from which any real hope for release is pure fantasy.[8] So repugnant is this picture that many have spent their lives attempting to repudiate it. Yet the logic seems irrevocable. If, as Lorenz declares, man does indeed share with lower life the instinct of aggression, this must to some degree color his cognitive vision for so long as he remains in his present evolutionary state.

Any student of behavior aware of our likenesses as well as our differences knows that man's extreme difficulty in accepting "rea-

son" outside the pale of his own dominant convictions and preju-
dices is a trait common to all men. For example, two people with
fundamentally different attitudes are able to agree on matters of
only trifling importance. If they are colleagues of long standing and
desirous of maintaining tolerable relations, they quickly map out the
danger zones and skirt them cautiously like two cats circling a bowl
of hot porridge. More than likely, the one will view the other as
something of a philistine or a fool, at least within these prescribed
areas, and must often remind himself of the other's legal claim to
voice opinions which seem to him disastrous. In such instances the
injunction that he respect the opinions of his fellowman is too much
to bear; it is enough that he grudgingly concede him the right to
express them.

It is enlightening when lifelong proponents of "reason," with
strongly differing viewpoints, take up cudgels against each other.
May I recommend to the reader, for an hour's entertainment, the
exchange of letters between the late Bertrand Russell and John Fish-
er, former senior editor of *Harper's* magazine, on the subject of
missile systems and thermonuclear warheads?[9] Of course, Russell's
position against the bomb had been an embattled one for a number
of years, so we may perhaps forgive him for the times when his
barbed witticisms got in the way of his arguments. But it really
makes little difference. In spite of the mass of evidence in support of
either position—indeed, because of it—one finds it impossible to
come away with any nucleus of fact to give either side the clean edge
of victory; the reader must simply take comfort in whatever he is
most disposed to believe.

It ends, as such controversies usually do, in a cul-de-sac of exacer-
bated feelings and blunt, heavy-sided arguments colliding head-on. In
all probability, neither man could have acquitted himself in any other way than he did. Inextricably bound in the mesh of his own style
of viewing life, each had embarked on a course whose outcome was
irreversible. As one psychologist concludes after a careful review of
the experimental data, "Facts have relatively little impact on the
man who has made up his mind. . . . It takes an overpowering array
of facts to change the minds of people who are set in a belief that has
emotional significance."[10]

It is not our intent to discredit the need for reason, nor to elevate
the position of emotions. Our thesis is simply that, because attitudes

function in the peculiar way they do, the emotions of young children must be made the primary target of public education, and the educator who wishes to improve the human condition without full recognition of this fact is merely whistling in the dark. He must be able to distinguish between attitudes which are liberating and those which are imprisoning; between the ones which most fully enable the child's imagination to range free and those which slam the door shut on him so that often he stands outside it, not even wondering what lies beyond. The educator must be made to realize that the imprisoned mind is, in some respects, as much the product of Scarsdale as it is of Harlem and that college credentials are by no means a guarantee against it. He must have some inkling, finally, of the forces which affect attitudes and the important principle under which these forces operate.

Unfortunately, our knowledge of such matters is still painfully limited. We know a great deal more, for example, about how to teach a highly complex idea, such as the relationship between climate and culture, than we do about instilling so simple a belief as integrity. Although research has shown us that attitudes can be formed or modified through a principle called identification, we are not at all sure what happens when identification takes place.

We do have some understanding, however, of one or two of its peculiarities and the conditions under which it is most apt to occur. We know that, unlike intellectualization, in which the gestalt of conceptual learning must be in large part independently achieved, the learning of an attitude seems to be far more an act of sheer dependence. Sometimes it may be dependence on the quality of experience which introduces the element of pleasure or pain. More often it is dependence on specific human models or types, either fictional or real, with which the learner establishes a strong emotional affinity and whose characteristic behaviors he uncritically accepts and makes a part of his own way of perceiving the world.[11]

Because identification takes on a major dimension in our problem, establishing an atmosphere most conducive to its operation is crucial. Such an atmosphere is achieved only through a number of uniquely *human* characteristics within the teacher and his curriculum. This sounds harmless enough, but in fact it contains ramifications which, when considered in their entirety, may be sources of embarrassment and trepidation.

Let us first of all look briefly at the teacher. In our scheme of things, if he were to possess but one dominant trait, it would be his spirit of reverence for children. Although this is a quality which hiring personnel widely subscribe to in theory, they make little effort in practice to insure its presence in the candidate and often give higher priority to scholarship and organizational ability. Yet, according to the eminent analyst, Erich Fromm, it not only stands as the single most important ingredient within the teacher's repertoire of personal characteristics, but is one which our own materialistic culture has largely ignored. In his own words, "While we teach knowledge, we are losing that teaching which is the most important one for human development: the teaching which can only be given by the simple presence of a mature, loving person. In previous epochs of our own culture, or in China and India, the man most highly valued was the person with outstanding spiritual qualities. Even the teacher was not only, or even primarily, a source of information, but his function was to convey certain human attitudes. . . ."[12]

But reverence for children by itself will not do; it is frequently too passive in character. What is needed, if things are to happen between teacher and pupil, are certain talents which serve as catalytic agents in a chemical reaction. High among these is the teacher as dramatist—not in the sense of the accomplished actor, but one skillfully trained to recognize those parts of the curriculum which lend themselves to dramatic treatment. I am not suggesting that we abandon the teaching of rational processes, but simply that we place them whenever possible within an emotional context, employing such elements as narrative, conflict, and denouement. In order for attitude formation to occur, teachers must espouse the arguments which favor the attitude we wish to instill.[13] If this seems like a hard saying, suggestive of indoctrination, we should perhaps re-examine the attitude in question, or abandon our efforts in this area entirely. What exerts the greatest impact on children's attitudes is not that their motivations, either rational or irrational, are exposed to reason, but that children are exposed to dynamic teachers.

In an age of vast social change and upheaval, the teacher as social critic is indispensable to the program. The notion that small children cannot identify with social issues involving the most fundamental human rights is sheer nonsense. Awakening children to feelings and attitudes which are couched in sophisticated language is not easy, but it is not impossible. What child has not felt the iron barb of rejection by his classmates or teacher through no fault of his own, or the panic fear that comes from having voiced an unpopular opinion, or the bitterness of isolation in a contest of unequal opportunity? These, it seems to me, are the very stuff on which human rights are built.

The teacher must also possess the temper of the liberal mind if his presence before children is not to exemplify a highly dogmatic and opinionated view of life. By the liberal attitude we mean one which is trusting and accepting of others, however bizarre their ideas or appearance, and unfearful of losing face when found wrong. It is the attitude which in turn enables children to express themselves, not anarchistically but fearlessly, so that they need not build insular detachments and hostilities in defense of their own errors, which so often lead to the narrow, prejudiced outlook. The learner whose responses are purposely disruptive, or who maintains frigid silence, is the product of teachers (and parents) who have themselves squirmed under the lash of the authoritarian's scorn.

Except for the temper of liberalism, which is sometimes sadly lacking in the very youth whose courage and dedication we so much admire, the teacher we speak of might well be drawn from the ranks of articulate young radicals. He might be something of a firebrand, uncomfortable to live with, a bane to his principal but a joy to his children, who see him as the champion of their own unredressed grievances against the adult world. Teachers who are the least popular with school boards and administrators are most frequently lionized in the classroom. Recently I witnessed a young professor ceremoniously announcing his resolution to resign if his department did not agree to changes which he firmly believed were imperative to the welfare of his students. A number of his colleagues considered such an announcement not only premature, but the benefits to be derived hardly worth the risk. The favorable impact on students, however, was instantaneous. Their roar of approval brought the house down. "He's a fool," I overheard one of his older colleagues whisper, "but he is enormously popular with these kids."

For the teacher deeply concerned with children's attitudes toward the world they live in, the style and content of much of today's elementary curriculum must be vaguely disappointing. Except for a small but growing volume of library fiction, the reading which takes up so large a part of the child's school time is quite devoid of all but the most innocuous kinds of social learning. The readers, especially at the lower elementary levels, are still largely occupied with community helpers, lost pets, animal characters, and trite mysteries. Apart from the occasional child's classic or story written by the established writer, their only claim to drama is that they employ the technique of dialogue whose banalities are frequently matched only by those of the plot. Much of a child's life is involved with misplaced puppies and make-believe journeys to the moon, but these cannot be the whole of it. Deep attachment, deep loss, hate, fear, rivalry, and revenge are as much a part of his life as they are of the adult's.

In response to the discovery that children of minority groups are conspicuously absent from the literary world of the white middle-class child, publishers are now hastening to fill in the gap. As we flip through the pages of their latest editions, we find increasing numbers of illustrations which begin to look suspiciously like characters from Negro, Chinese, and Mexican families.[14] But although the children's eyes are slanted or their skins dark, one would never dream that the black child had a single problem that was significantly, or even mildly, different from his white classmate's. Together they walk the shaded streets of suburbia, wearing the same clothes and playing the same games. Inside bright new homes they enjoy sumptuous holiday dinners and lavish yuletide gifts—all remarkably similar. There is no anguish or pain. Segregation, isolation, racism—indeed anything that smacks of the privation or privilege found in the lives of real children —have been carefully deleted from their world, leaving it sparkling, aseptic, and trouble-free.

Elementary social studies suffer from a different kind of illness, but it leads essentially to the same result. Expository writing, concept building, and the integration of new disciplines dominate their pages to the exclusion of social themes which, if mentioned at all, receive but scant attention. This does not mean that they lack scholarship. Indeed, the author with the Ph.D. in history appears with increasing frequency on the title pages. The one criticism we cannot make is their want of dedication to their own brand of "truth."

But for the child whose impressions are yet unformed (above the elementary levels, traditional historical approaches are quite acceptable), the importance of historical themes lies in *how* the stories are told. To illustrate, let us turn for the moment to the standard treatment of the Indian. In one volume,[15] deference is paid to Chief

Joseph and his tribe for having been badly used by our government. In the space of a few pages we learn all the "objective" facts about our comparative cultures, Joseph's brilliance as an Indian general, and his retirement onto a reservation, "a wise and gentle leader of his people."[16] Interesting as the facts might be, they may well have been left unsaid. Of infinitely more importance for the young child's mind is that Chief Joseph should serve as a symbol of our treatment of minority groups. In this use of history, children glimpse the haunting loveliness of the Wallowa valley, the ancestral home of the Nez Percé tribe. They observe the incredible greed of miners and pioneers, followed by swift encroachment, dishonored treaties, and a long list of indignities which at last force upon Joseph his momentous decision to fight.

While his remarkable generalship in a long series of running battles is high drama, its chief importance lies in the specific details. Children should know something of Chief Joseph's anguish as he watches the slow and systematic extermination of his people. Through his eyes and ears they should be made to look upon defenseless women and children ruthlessly put to the sword by U.S. troops, and hear the children's whimpering cries of hunger, pain, and cold as the embattled tribe, ever on the move, fights its way over 1,500 tortuous miles of wilderness in advance of the pursuing U.S. army. Perhaps then they might gain some understanding of the tragic depth of Chief Joseph's resignation and bitterness as he makes his surrendering speech—one of the most simple and moving in Indian oratory: "I am tired of fighting. Our chiefs are killed. Looking Glass is dead. Tu-hul-hut-sut is dead. The old men are all dead. . . . It is cold and we have no blankets. The little children are freezing to death. I want to have time to look for my children and see how many of them I can find. Maybe I shall find them among the dead. Hear me, my chiefs. . . . From where the sun now stands I will fight no more forever."[17]

Nor should children be spared the last act of perfidy in this drama, when our government, in violation of the solemn pledge upon which Chief Joseph laid down his arms, condemned him and the tattered remnant of his tribe to a strange and hostile environment nearly 2,000 miles away, where eight years of neglect and disease reduced his small group to a tiny handful.

For small children this is one of a number of precious themes in a great heritage involving man's continuing battle for human rights.

What a pity to squander it as we do. The fact that it shames our honor makes it no less significant, but rather more so. How else can we develop in our children a sense of national conscience? What better way to insure that such barbarism, of which our government is from time to time capable, should never happen again?

It is curious that those branches of the federal government, which so generously dispense their largess on a confusing array of research projects, have never enlisted the aid of the gifted dramatist to help write the curriculum for the needs of the child's emotional world. Indeed, the idea of a calculated approach to the problem may bear upon factors of which we are only now becoming aware. Robert Ardrey's thesis, for example, that much of our most morally despicable behavior is genetically, rather than socially, stimulated[18] must compel us to take a fresh look at the way educational institutions attempt to socialize our offspring—a system consisting in no small degree of repressive conditioning techniques which are leading, for all we know, to a kind of vast social neurosis. If this has any basis in truth, alternatives must be found which enable children to "work out" instinctive behavior under controlled circumstances. Psychologists now tell us that even dreams help serve the important function of defusing our conflicts and go on to predict dire consequences if this capacity were to be seriously inhibited. Fantasy in some form, whether through dreams, suggestive techniques, or the world of dramatic literature, holds an important key to mental health and, hence, to the liberating of reflective processes. It is to this end that public education must direct its efforts if we are to come within shouting distance of the humanist's ideal of rational man.

Notes

1. John H. Bunzel, "What's Happening to Democracy?" *Saturday Review* (May 17, 1969), 28-29.

2. *Ibid.*, 28.

3. *Ibid.*, 29.

4. John Bowlby, *Maternal Care and Mental Health* (Geneva: World Health Organization, Monograph Series No. 2, 1951).

5. Desmond Morris, *The Naked Ape* (New York: Dell Publishing Co., 1969).

6. Konrad Lorenz, *On Aggression* (New York: Bantam Books, 1967).

7. Robert Ardrey, *African Genesis* (New York: Dell Publishing Co., 1969). Mr. Ardrey, who took his academic training in the natural sciences, became a successful playwright and screenwriter.

8. Morris, *op. cit.*, 9. This theme generally persists throughout the book.

9. "Bertrand Russell on the Sinful Americans: A Somewhat Frustrating Exchange of Letters," *Harper's* (June 1963), 20-26.

10. Lee J. Cronbach, *Educational Psychology* (New York: Harcourt, Brace & World, 1963), 449.

11. Ives Hendrick, *Facts and Theories of Psychoanalysis* (New York: Alfred A. Knopf, 1958), 156-67.

12. Erich Fromm, *The Art of Loving* (New York: Harper & Row, Bantam Books, 1963), 98.

13. Muzafer Sherif and Carolyn W. Sherif, *An Outline of Social Psychology* (New York: Harper and Brothers, 1956), 560. The authors describe an experiment in which specific attitudes emerge only when the teacher "draws conclusions" for learners rather than leaving an issue suspended between several alternatives.

14. I examined the Lippincott, Follett, Macmillan, and McGraw-Hill readers. There are probably some others.

15. Joseph S. Junell, *Exploring the Northwest* (Chicago: Follett Publishing Company, 1966).

16. *Ibid.*, 81-82.

17. *Ibid.*

18. Ardrey, *op. cit.*, 321-64. This is one of several themes that run through his book, but it is most prominent in his chapter entitled "Cain's Children."

7. Transcendence and the Curriculum

Philip H. Phenix

The purpose of this paper is to show the significance of transcendence for the interpretation and evaluation of educational theory and practice. I shall begin by stating what is meant by this concept, indicating certain allied and contrasting ideas, and analyzing several dimensions of experience to which it pertains. I shall then apply the concept, showing its relation to a number of general dispositions that are important in teaching and learning. Finally, I shall suggest somewhat more specifically the consequences for the curriculum that flow from acknowledging and celebrating transcendence.

The method used in this analysis may be characterized as both phenomenological and empirical. It is phenomenological in that I endeavor to categorize certain phases of human consciousness as immediately presented in introspection. It is empirical in that throughout an appeal is made to human experience, without recourse to supernatural interventions, or, if the latter are to be acknowledged, that their meaning is to be interpreted in terms of experiential categories. Thus I am engaging in what is customarily called natural theology, as distinguished from revealed theology. I do not begin

Reprinted with permission of the author and of *Teachers College Record* (73 [December 1971], 271-83).

with a presumed commitment to the faith of a given historic community, but with what I presume to be universal or universalizable
experiences, the analysis of which is open to the scrutiny of natural
reason.

I confess that there is a faith underlying these reflections, and that
it probably consists of a certain cluster of commitments and primordial persuasions that have their genesis in the life of the community
of learning as I have experienced it. Accordingly, this effort may be
regarded as the explication of what I consider to be certain faith
presuppositions of the educative community, utilizing some of the
conceptual apparatus of modern philosophical natural theology, with
deductive elaborations to show what educational aims and practices
are coherent with those presuppositions.

The Meaning of Transcendence

Transcendence may be regarded as the most characteristic concept
for the interpretation of religious phenomena. Religious experience is
the experience of transcendence. Note that I do not say "experience
of the transcendent," implying an object which an experiencing subject apprehends. I prescind from the ontological question at this
point in order to concentrate on the phenomenology of the immediate experience of transcending. It is not that the ontological question
is unimportant or irrelevant. I prescind from it because the experience of transcendence is the necessary starting point for formulating
the meaning of any ontological assertions and because I am convinced that the being of transcendence embraces and unites what are
called objectivity and subjectivity.

The term "transcendence" refers to the experience of limitless
going beyond any given state or realization of being. It is an inherent
property of conscious being to be aware that every concrete entity is
experienced within a context of wider relationships and possibilities.
Conscious life is always open to a never-ending web of entailments
and unfoldings. No content of experience is just what it appears to
be here and now without any further prospects or associations. All
experience is characterized by an intrinsic dynamism that in principle
breaks every bound that rational patterning or practical convenience
may establish.

The sense of this fundamental category can perhaps be made clearer by referring to some of the cognate terms that have been employed in the theological tradition to point to it. The one most akin is infinitude, which expresses the never-finished enlargement of contexts within which every bounded entity is enmeshed. To affirm the finiteness of anything is to presuppose a participation in infinitude that makes it possible to acknowledge the finite. Finitude is thus a specification of limitation within the ambience of infinitude—a deliberate stemming of transcendence for purposes of conceptual or active control.

A second allied concept is spirit. Spirit is the name given to the property of limitless going beyond. To have a spiritual nature is to participate in infinitude. Reason refers to the capacity for the rational ordering of experience through categories of finitude. Spirit makes one aware of the finiteness of the structures imposed by reason. To say that persons are beings with spirit is to point to their perennial discontent and dissatisfaction with any and every finite realization. Thus it is sometimes said that spirit finds its exemplification more in the yearning impulses of feeling and the innovative projects of will than in the settled conclusions of intellect.

The essential quality of transcendence is manifest also in the secular concept of idealization, which is central, for example, in the nontheistic, naturalistic thought of John Dewey. Every actuality is set within a context of ideal possibility. Every end realized becomes the means for the fulfillment of further projected ideals, and this is a process that is generic to human experience. Much the same idea is implicit in Dewey's concept of continuous growth—of that valuable growth that leads to further growth. The qualitative test of growth is whether it is consistent with a limitless enrichment of realizations through the progressive actualization of ideal possibilities. This vision of continuous, progressive reconstruction of experience as the norm of human existence is a nontheological interpretation of the fundamental religious concept of transcendence.

Dimensions of Transcendence

The general concept of transcendence may be analyzed into at least three principal dimensions: temporal, extensive, and qualitative. Temporal transcendence refers to infinitude of process. The experience of temporal passage in its essence is a consciousness of transcendence, for it manifests an ineluctable going beyond. Herodotus was the first among Western thinkers to point to the primordial character of temporal flux, within which the logos of reason was a subordinate principle of order. In modern philosophy, Bergson was perhaps the foremost exponent of the basic dynamism of reality, which he called the *élan vital,* apprehended by an act of intuition that yields profounder insight than the static conceptions of discursive reason. Whitehead also made "creative advances into novelty," i.e, continuous temporal transcendence, the most fundamental presupposition of his system of categories for describing reality.

To be humanly alive is to experience each moment as a new creation, to know that this moment, though continuous with the past, is yet a distinct and fresh emergence, which will in turn yield to still further novel realizations. Every human present, retrospectively regarded, is perceived as created, and prospectively regarded, as a destiny. These two terms—creation and destiny—are the two temporal poles between which transcendence ranges. As such, they are perennially important theological categories. The experiential meaning of creation—of being created—is the consciousness of retrospective temporal transcendence of prior states of being. The experiential meaning of destiny, and of participating in creative activity, is the consciousness of prospective actualizations beyond every particular attainment. The various ideas in the religions of mankind referring to the preexistence or immortality of the soul aim to symbolize the temporal dimension of transcendence both in its retrospective and prospective modes.

A second dimension of transcendence is extension. Limitless going beyond is experienced not only with reference to time but also in respect to inclusiveness. The classic philosophical statement of this dimension of transcendence is supplied by the doctrine of internal relations, which is the central idea and the key to philosophical idealism, though not exclusively wedded to that way of thinking. According to this doctrine, any entity is constituted by the set of relationships that it has with all other entities. Thus nothing exists in isolation, but always in relation. Reality is a single interconnected whole, such that the complete description of any entity would require the comprehension of every other entity.

One influential formulation of the principle of extensive transcendence is found in Whitehead's Philosophy of Organism, in the concept of "ingredience." According to Whitehead's system, the ingredients that go into the constitution of every event include all other past events, each apprehended according to an appropriate measure of relevance. Hence every actual occasion or event is a particular mirroring of the whole universe.

Something of the same idea is implicit in modern field theories and in the ideas of contextualism and ecology. An electron, a magnet, a chunk of matter, or a person is never an isolated, separate entity, but exists in a context of electrostatic, magnetic, gravitational, or personal field relationships. In the last analysis, every being is a being-in-relation, and is what it is and behaves as it does by virtue of its participation with other beings.

The theological expression of the principle of extensive transcendence is supplied by the doctrine of monotheism and of the divine omnipresence. There is a single ultimate ground of all being, and all beings are mutually related in that common unitary reality. Hence, every particular experience contains the possibility of evincing the limitless wealth of participations to which it is heir, thereby bearing witness to a principle of transcendence toward wholeness that is one hallmark of religious orientation.

To the temporal and extensive dimensions of transcendence a third may be added, namely the qualitative. This dimension refers to the consciousness of limitless possibility of going beyond in degrees of excellence. It is the source of the principle of criticism that levies judgments of relative worth on concrete actualizations. What this principle affirms is that no actual occasion or finite grouping of occasions constitutes a complete qualitative achievement, but that beyond all such realizations higher fulfillments are possible.

This dimension of qualitative transcendence is well exemplified in one of the central concepts in Tillich's theology, that is, in what he terms the "Protestant Principle." By this term he does not refer primarily to the historic movement called Protestantism, but rather to the principle of protest that denies qualitative ultimacy to any actuality, be it institution, person, belief, or cultural norm. According to this principle, the religious consciousness is manifest in the refusal to accord supreme worth to any and every realization of nature or humanity. Implicit in such refusal is commitment to an inexhaustible ideality that renders a judgment of partiality and insufficiency on whatever exists.

The theological expression of qualitative transcendence is also contained in such concepts as divine holiness, righteousness, and perfection. That God is holy, righteous, and perfect experientially signifies the persuasion of the human consciousness that no finite reality is of supreme worth, the creative restlessness of the human spirit that never remains content with any historic attainment, and the perennial protest of the prophetic conscience against the absolutizing of limited goods.

Universality and Negation of Transcendence

It has been suggested that transcendence is a primordial category for the interpretation of human experience in the sense that it is an elemental and ineluctable aspect of the human condition. That is to say that transcendence is universal. It is phenomenologically not the case that some persons, called "religious" or "spiritual" types, experience it while others do not. I am arguing that human consciousness is rooted in transcendence, and that analysis of all human consciousness discloses the reality of transcendence as a fundamental presupposition of the human condition. To be sure, this same human consciousness also discloses aspects of finitude. Acts of demarcation, of limitation, and of closure are manifestly present in human behavior. What I maintain is that all such finite determinations are imbedded in and are specifications of an indeterminate ground of creative advance into novelty, of contextual relations, and of qualitative gradations.

The relation of finite and infinite in man has the paradoxical property that boundless creative lures, outreachings for wider relations, and strivings for ideality, all of which transcendent tensions challenge the status quo of finite realizations, cause persons to negate transcendence in order to save themselves from the threatened dissolution of actual attainments. The denial of spirituality in the name of individual self-sufficiency or various forms of absolutism, of institution, race, class, nation, tradition, or doctrine, is evidence of this flight from transcendence. This negative self-protective movement is what the Judaic and Christian traditions have called sin. As theologians in these traditions have regularly pointed out, the pervasive and persistent denial of transcendence is, in fact, prime evidence for the presence and power of transcendence. This is the meaning of the myth that portrays the devil as a fallen angel, that is, as a spiritual agent employing his creative transcendence to generate an illusion of self-sufficing autonomy.

General Dispositions

We are now in a position to proceed with a discussion of the significance of the experience of transcendence for the enterprise of education. Certain qualities of life are associated with transcendence, and at the same time play a decisive role in teaching and learning. I submit that these general human dispositions provide a set of criteria for a transcendence-oriented curriculum as contrasted with one that is predicated upon the neglect or denial of transcendence.

Hope

The first disposition engendered by the experience of transcendence is hope. Hope is the mainspring of human existence. As existentialist thinkers remind us, conscious life is a continual projection into the future. Even though the adventure may project one into the unknown, it is animated by an affirmation of the movement forward in time. Without hope, there is no incentive for learning, for the impulse to learn presupposes confidence in the possibility of improving one's existence. It can be argued that widespread loss of hope is one of the principal causes of the educational problems that beset contemporary America. When widespread social dislocations, dissolution of customary norms, dehumanization, and other malaises of social and cultural life cause people to feel impotent, no technical improvements in the content or methods of instruction will induce people to learn well. On the other hand, those who are buoyed by strong hope can overcome substantial formal deficiencies in program or technique. The explicit acknowledgment of transcendence as a ground for hope may therefore contribute significantly to the efficacy of education.

Few recent thinkers have so persuasively argued that a transcendent hope is the driving force for personal and collective achievement as Teilhard de Chardin. He saw the cultural and educational crisis of our time primarily as a faltering of hope; by presenting a cosmological vision in which man's conscious responsible striving for progress is viewed as continuous with the upward drive toward coordination that has powered the entire evolutionary ascent, he endeavored to provide intellectual warrant for an animating hope that can give mankind the heart to continue learning.

Creativity

The recognition of transcendence as inseparable from the human condition lends special emphasis to the disposition toward creativity. To be human is to create. The fashioning of new constructs is not an exceptional activity reserved for a minority of gifted persons; it is rather the normal mode of behavior for everyone. Dull repetitiveness and routinism are evidences of dehumanization. In this respect the institutions and practices of education have often inhibited, rather than fostered, humaneness, by inculcating habits of automatic conformity instead of imaginative origination.

The prime enemy of creativity is the flight from transcendence which in the theological tradition of the West has been termed sin. Insofar as educators function as agents for transmitting and confirming cultural traditions unchanged, they are ministers of sin. When they presume to act as authorities dispensing to the young knowledge and values that are to be accepted without question, they act as enemies of transcendence. On the other hand, the educator who affirms transcendence is characterized by a fundamental humility manifest in expectant openness to fresh creative possibilities. To be sure, he does not ignore or discount the funded wisdom of the past. He does not regard it as a fixed patrimony to be preserved, but as a working capital for investment in the projects of an unfolding destiny.

Creativity is fostered by having due regard both for transcendence and for immanence. By the experience of immanence I mean the sense of importance in what is actualized in existence. Immanence and transcendence are intimately related. Immanence is the treasure deposited by the creative activity of transcendence. Existential realizations lose their savor when the freshness of transcendent impulse that ushered in their birth is forgotten, and projected enterprises degenerate into quixotic gestures when the sustaining and ennobling structures of past actualizations are rejected. The educator thus fosters creativity when he loves and respects the traditional learning, conceived as immanence, to be transformed and rejuvenated in the service of transcendence.

Awareness

The dispositions of hope and creativity correspond to the temporal dimension of transcendence. Corresponding to the extensive dimension are the dispositions of awareness: sympathy, empathy, hospitality, and tolerance, that is to say, openness outwards, as well as toward the future. In acknowledging transcendence, one adopts a positive attitude toward all other persons, other cultures, and other social groups, in fact, toward all other beings, including the objects of nature. Accepting transcendence frees one from the self-protecting isolation that regards the different or the unfamiliar as a threat to be avoided. Alienation is evidence of the flight from transcendence, and separation and exclusion are manifestations of the primary sin of striving for self-sufficient autonomy.

No teaching can occur without a predisposition toward relation on the part of the teacher who seeks to shape the life of the student and to mediate to the student his (the teacher's) life of relation with the circumambient world. Nor will the student learn effectively in the absence of a hospitable openness to that world and to those who assist him in establishing satisfying relationships with it. This factor of sensitivity is the main theme in Buber's pedagogical theory. For him, the clue to significant education does not reside in the specific methods or contents of instruction, but in the presupposition of the primacy and the power of the elemental relation, which is the source of all being. He sees the primordial relation as a reality in which one may confidently dwell, and within which the particular categories and connections of reason and practice are secondarily discriminated. This assumed indwelling by the teacher in transcendence can help to release the student's powers of awareness, thus providing strong catalysis for learning. In turn, teachers who are inured to self-defensive closedness may be liberated to wider sympathies by sharing in the relatively unspoiled freshness of young people who affirm the world and celebrate the possibilities of ever-deepening relationships within it.

Doubt and Faith

Corresponding to the qualitative dimension of transcendence are the twin dispositions of constructive doubt and faith or, combining the two, faithful doubt. A central insight of Tillich's thought is this intimate linkage of doubt and faith within the context of transcendence. Tillich argues that really serious doubt—the radical questioning of any and every alleged finality—is only possible to one who is grasped by a transcendent faith, that is, who enjoys a confidence that wells up from the creative grounds of being and does not rest on any objectified security structures. This position is summarized in Tillich's reformulation of Luther's doctrine of justification by faith in the state of sin to read justification by faith in the state of doubt. The serious doubter is justified by his faith in the unconditioned ground of being manifest in the very seriousness of his activity of doubting.

The educator rooted in transcendence helps to foster a constructive disposition toward doubt, that is, a spirit of criticism. Such a spirit is to be distinguished sharply from the destructive doubt of the cynic or skeptic or from the attitude of indifference engendered by dilettante sophistication. The latter dispositions are essentially faithless, in the sense that they presuppose the futility of any sustained quest for truth or right on the grounds that the perennial struggle of mankind to achieve demonstrable securities has proven unsuccessful. Abandoning the search for ultimate certainties, the skeptic unwittingly cuts the ground from under serious inquiry itself, thus discrediting even his own activity of doubting. The Cartesian insight still holds, though in modified form: I doubt, therefore I am. The secure foundation of the human condition as a spiritual being is the faith-evidencing activity of concerned and responsible doubting.

The teacher who is spiritually aware does not seek to protect himself from the insecurity of uncertainty, perplexity, and irremediable ignorance. He does not try to hide behind a screen of academic presumption and professional expertise, embellished with mystifying jargon. Nor does he confuse the role of teacher with that of authoritative oracle. He does not expect or encourage his students supinely to accept his beliefs or directions. On the other hand, he shares with conviction and enthusiasm the light that he believes he possesses, and encourages his students to do the same, resolutely resisting in himself and in his students the paralysis and sense of futility associated with skepticism and indifference.

Wonder, Awe, and Reverence

Consummating the dispositions associated with the experience of transcendence are the attitudes of wonder, awe, and reverence. Consciousness of infinitude entails a sense of the manifold powers and possibilities of the reality in which one's existence is embedded. This sense is the root of the impulse to learn. Dewey spoke of the unsolved problem as the stimulus for thought. I believe his concept of the problem as basically the blocking of organic drives was too narrowly biological, and that a sounder, more positive, and more distinctly human formulation would be that thought grows out of wonder, which in turn is rooted in the spiritual act of projecting ideal possibilities. Thus instead of regarding human learning primarily as a means of biological adaptation, it may be thought of as a response to the lure of transcendence. Indeed, the very notion of adaptation appears to be meaningful only in terms of the process of creative invention for the purpose of realizing specific ideal harmonies.

Wonder refers to the suspenseful tension of consciousness toward the unknown future in response to the attraction of unrealized potentialities. It includes the vague adumbration of enriching relationships yet unestablished but beckoning. It is the hovering shadow of an answer resident in every question seriously asked. Awe is the sense of momentousness excited by the experience of transcendence. It is the source of persistent interest in learning and of patient efforts toward realization, born of the sense that the human career, as well as the cosmic enterprise of which it is a part, is an affair of capital importance. Reverence betokens a recognition of one's participation in transcendence as a surprising and continually renewed gift, in contrast to the view of one's existence as a secure possession and as an autonomous achievement. The reverent disposition saves one from the arrogance of self-sufficiency which interferes with openness to creative possibilities in learning, and issues in a spirit of thankfulness for the gift of life that makes study a welcome opportunity and not a chore and an obligation.

Consequences for the Curriculum

The acknowledgment of transcendence suggests a curriculum that has due regard for the uniqueness of the human personality. If a person is a creative subject, then the core of his selfhood can never be defined in terms of objective formative patterns that are common to a social group. To be sure, for practical purposes provision must be made to enable the young to participate effectively in the common life. But it makes a great difference whether the patterns of culture are regarded as essentially constitutive of the personality or as resources for use by a personality whose springs of being lie at a deeper level than any social norm, that is to say, in transcendence.

A curriculum of transcendence provides a context for engendering, gestating, expecting, and celebrating the moments of singular awareness and of inner illumination when each person comes into the consciousness of his inimitable personal being. It is not characterized so much by the objective content of studies as by the atmosphere created by those who comprise the learning community. Its opposite is the engineering outlook that regards the learner as material to be formed by means of a variety of technical procedures. In contrast, the curriculum of transcendence requires a context of essential freedom, though not of anarchy, which is the correlate of indifference and of skepticism about the structures of being. Freedom in the school of transcendence is based on openness to fresh possibilities of insight and invention and provision of ample cultural and interpersonal resources for the formation of unique structures of existence.

Concern for Wholeness

The lure of transcendence is toward wholeness. It follows that the educator in responding to that incitement creates a curriculum that fosters comprehensiveness of experience. The argument for education of the whole person in the last analysis rests on the consciousness of transcendence. In a technical, success-oriented society the payoff is found in specialized competence. From the standpoint of personal and social efficiency, the arguments for breadth of knowledge and skill are few and unconvincing. To be sure, there must be some with sufficient scope of understanding to be able to coordinate the parts of the social mechanism. Yet even their comprehensiveness can be conceived in narrow managerial terms. The case for general education for all rests finally on the nature of persons as essentially constituted by the hunger for wholeness.

A curriculum designed to respond to this hunger is obviously multidisciplinary. It affords opportunities for the enrichment of understanding in diverse areas of human experience, as, for example, in the theoretical, the practical, and the affective domains. Narrowness and exclusivity of concentration are incompatible with the demands of transcendence.

On the other hand, it is important not to be misled into the advocacy of superficial generality in the plan of studies. Since transcendence has a qualitative as well as an extensive dimension, it is just as essential to provide opportunities for intensive understanding as for extensive range of studies. That is why the curriculum of transcendence is multidisciplinary in nature. The disciplinary character insures depth of penetration—a progressive enlargement of insight within the framework of methods and categories that has proven fruitful in inquiry. It cannot be overemphasized that transcendence is not simply openness-in-general. It presupposes that being has structures. These structures are the immanent patterns of transcendence. Hence, the necessity for discipline. Transcendence is not an invitation to anarchy but to glad obedience to the structures or logos of being. These patterns are the objective norms for knowledge and for conduct, and they are what the various disciplines aim to disclose. Productiveness of insight in any discipline is evidence that the categories and procedures that define it in some degree reflect the logos of being.

The criterion of wholeness, then, is not incompatible with specialized inquiry. It does, however, require that each specialized mode of investigation be understood in relation to other such modes. Each discipline is founded upon certain deliberate limitations and simplifications which make it possible to advance understanding of inexhaustibly complex realities. What consciousness of transcendence does is to make one aware of the partiality of each disciplined outlook and sensitive to the many-sidedness of the reality that one confronts. Recognition of partiality of perspective is evidence of a more comprehensive perspective from which the judgment of partiality is rendered. Transcendence leads to the acknowledgment that the truth of any discipline mode is never the whole truth, and to active interest in the relationships and complementarities among the various disciplines. In this sense, the curriculum in the light of transcendence is *inter*disciplinary as well as multidisciplinary.

Thus the awareness of transcendence provides justification for a broad and variegated curriculum securely grounded in the specialized disciplines. Studies are pursued in depth according to the tested methods of these disciplines, yet always with an eye to the similarities and contrasts with other disciplines and in full awareness of the need for complementation by alternative perspectives. Furthermore, though the various disciplines are conceived as channels of insight into the structures of being, it is not assumed that any standard or traditional set of disciplines provides the full and final disclosure of the nature of things. Hence consciousness of transcendence encourages an open-textured orientation toward the very enterprise of discipline making, hospitality toward the emergence of fresh discipline perspectives, and willingness to replace partial outlooks that have served well in the past with more comprehensive or penetrating ones as they emerge in the successive transformations in the evolution of culture. On these grounds, the transcendence-oriented educator helps his students to be alert to the realities of intellectual mutations, revolutions, and inventions, and endeavors to create an atmosphere and an expectation in which his students may share in the construction of new and more illuminating patterns of thought.

Education for Inquiry

The recognition of transcendence suggests a characteristic perception of the central task of teaching and learning as dedication to the practice of inquiry. The transcendent perspective is opposed to all outlooks that presuppose a fixed content of knowledge, beliefs, or skills that the learner is meant to acquire. The assumption that anything is knowable with completeness and certainty arrests inquiry and closes the channels that lead on to deeper and wider insight.

On the other hand, transcendence is compatible with confident acceptance of the possibility of valid knowledge, once its partial, limited, and contingent character is acknowledged. Inquiry then includes as an essential element the charting of these contextual limitations and the careful definition of the boundaries by which particular perspectives are characterized.

Commitment to inquiry is thus opposed to two polar positions: dogmatic finality or certainty and nihilistic skepticism about the possibility of warranted knowledge. The confident practice of inquiry rests on faith in the intelligibility of reality together with an acknowledgment of the boundless depth and the interconnections of the structures of intelligibility.

The orientation toward inquiry is one of the widely recognized aspects of recent curricular theory and practice and need not be described in any detail here. My intent in the present essay is only to show how this particular curriculum emphasis is related to the consciousness of transcendence and to suggest that it has its source and sustenance in that awareness.

The Practice of Dialogue

Inherent also in education carried on according to the norms of transcendence is the practice of dialogue. The extensive dimension of transcendence presupposes a lure toward ever wider associations of complementarity and of enriching relatedness. It is incompatible with all self-sufficient isolation and exclusiveness of perspective. Hence growth in understanding is to be sought by engaging in the activity of open-ended, continuing communication. The indissoluble unity between teaching and learning is affirmed in the recognition that enlargement and refinement of insight are possible only through the mutual stimulation of conjoint inquiry. One learns effectively only as he seeks to make his perspectives intelligible to others and in turn seeks to enter into their perceptions. A practical consequence of this insight for the curriculum maker is that he organize the teaching-learning enterprise with maximum provision for dialogic activity. Such activity consists of more than mere conversation or discussion. Real dialogue is a high skill requiring sympathetic and practical leadership based upon the will to communicate which in turn is founded on the capacity to enter sympathetically and expectantly into the minds of other persons, which capacity is evidence of transcendence.

The Cultivation of Transcendence

In the foregoing I have sought to explicate the concept "transcendence" as a fundamental category for interpreting human experience and to suggest some of the relationships of this concept to the process of education. I have indicated that some important human values have their roots in transcendence, and I have argued that transcendence is the basic presupposition of a certain set of curricular goals and styles. Insofar, then, as one is committed to these values and educational aims, it is natural, in concluding such an exposition and analysis as this, to inquire how the experience of transcendence may be cultivated so as to foster the desired educational realizations.

I answer this question with four points. First, there is a sense in which the consciousness of transcendence cannot be cultivated, since according to the position set forth here it is an inescapable reality of human existence. To exist is to participate in transcendence. Infinitude is essential, not accidental, in the being of persons. One may deny transcendence, but, as I have claimed, the very act of denial bears witness to it. Accordingly, transcendence simply *is,* and is not an option to be elected or rejected as a component of human experience.

Nonetheless, in the second place, cultivation of transcendence is possible in the sense that one learns to accept and welcome it and to live in the strength and illumination of it. The primary way to affirm it is by the practice of the life that stems from it. Thus, by living hopefully and creatively, with faith and reverence, by experiencing the joys of responsible freedom, by seeking for wholeness of disciplined understanding, and by engaging in continual dialogic inquiry, one tacitly acknowledges the presence and power of transcendence.

Third, an important factor in the cultivation of transcendence is the witness of those who consciously celebrate it in their own existence. When fearful and self-protecting tendencies tend to obscure the light of infinitude and doubts tend to annihilate rather than transform, one may bolster flagging faith by turning to others in strong grasp of transcendence. In this respect the teacher by his own mute witness may play a central role in the maintenance of the primordial grounds of learning morale.

Fourth, and finally, the awareness of transcendence may be clarified and fortified by articulating conceptual tools for describing and interpreting this fundamental experience. Such conceptual articulation provides a kind of rational justification for the basic presuppositions by which one lives. When the fundamental grounds of existence are made explicit in this way, they may be less subject to erosion by the forces of irrational fear and self-defensiveness than if they remain purely tacit. Thus philosophical theology of education, of which the present essay is intended to be an illustration, may contribute to the nurture of the awareness of transcendence and to the curricular consequences that are associated with it.

Selected References for Curriculum as a Means to Self-Actualization

Dinkmeyer, Don. "Top Priority: Understanding Self and Others," *Elementary School Journal* 72 (November 1971), 62-71.

Duckworth, Eleanor. "The Having of Wonderful Ideas," *Harvard Educational Review* 42 (May 1972), 217-31.

Greene, Maxine. "The Arts in a Global Village," *Educational Leadership* 26 (Fall 1969), 439-46.

_____ "Curriculum and Consciousness," *Teachers College Record* 73 (December 1971), 253-69.

Kirschner, J. "Education as Technology: Implications from the History of an Idea," *Teachers College Record* 70 (November 1968), 121-26.

Long, B. E., and D. Walsh. "Projective Education for the Child's Need to Know," *Social Education* 35 (March 1971), 295-300.

Maslow, Abraham. "Some Educational Implications, the Humanistic Psychologies," *Harvard Educational Review* 38 (Fall 1968), 685-96.

Pilder, William F. "Curriculum Design and the Knowledge Situation," *Educational Leadership* 26 (March 1969), 593-601.

_____ "Unlearning the Idea of School," *Educational Leadership* 28 (March 1971), 601-603.

Scriven, Michael. "Education for Survival," in K. Ryan and J. Cooper, (eds.), *Kaleidoscope* (Boston: Houghton Mifflin, 1972), 272-99.

Stern, George C. "Self-actualizing Environments for Students," *School Review* 80 (November 1971), 1-26.

Part Four
Curriculum for
Social Reconstruction-Relevance

Social reconstructionists see schooling as an agency of social change, and they demand that education be relevant both to the student's interests and to society's needs. Curriculum is conceived to be an active force having direct impact on the whole fabric of its human and social context. The four chapters in this section offer variations on this theme of relevance. Metcalf and Hunt (Chapter 8) discuss one current symptom of social imbalance—youth's rejection of the adult culture—and urge that this conflict be incorporated into the curriculum as subject matter. In Chapter 9, John Mann argues similarly for including a social issue in the curriculum (in this case, experience in the exercise of political power), less as a topic of discussion than as direct experience.

In Chapter 10 the focus shifts from the question of individual relevance and curriculum content to a more macro view of education as an agent of general social change. Harold Shane's article provides a social reconstructionist set of educational goals and, in its implicit critique of society, gives a different kind of answer to the question posed by Junnell in Chapter 6.

8. Relevance and the Curriculum

Lawrence E. Metcalf and *Maurice P. Hunt*

Our assignment in this article is to indicate what we mean by a relevant curriculum. We shall define curriculum not as "all the experiences a child or youth has in school" but more traditionally as "the formal course work taken by students." We believe that formal course work acquires relevance whenever it impinges upon what students believe, and whenever it has the effect of producing a pattern of belief that is well grounded and internally consistent.

Ours is a period of history in which youth on a mass and international scale rejects the culture of the old. This rejection is not universal to all youth; some are more actively opposed to established traditions; many are in tacit support of changes initiated by the bolder and more aggressive young. To a large extent the rebellion of the young began with college students, has now been adopted by large numbers of high school students, and is beginning to filter down into junior high school. Young people are beginning to develop their own culture, and appear at times to learn more from one another than from teachers or parents. Some adults feel so turned off and rejected that they doubt that they can ever say anything that youth would accept as relevant.

Reprinted from *Phi Delta Kappan* 51 (March 1970), 358-61, with permission of the authors and Phi Delta Kappa.

Youth's rejection of adult culture—"the whole, rotten, stinking mess of it"—has become a significant social movement. This movement has assumed international proportions; practically every modern, industrialized nation has felt its impact. Any school that has not made this social movement a subject of serious study on the part of its youthful clientele is about as irrelevant as it can get.

Rejection of adult culture is proclaimed overtly, not merely by verbal attack but also by deliberate adoption of grooming habits or display of those artifacts which have been established or promoted as symbols of sophisticated rebellion. New hair styles, manners of dress, a new language (which relies heavily on traditional Anglo-Saxon monosyllables), a new music, an open sexual promiscuity, and the use of drugs or pot—all reflect a wholesale rejection of tradition and orthodoxy.

Many of the new values and customs are carefully chosen as goads to older persons. "What would my parents or grandparents least like to have me think and see me do?" When this question has been answered, often only after some tests of adult reaction, the young then adopt whatever they think will best demonstrate that they are not part of the main culture stream of earlier generations. In the case of males, it may require only long hair and a string of beads to make the point. For females, attendance at a love-in or rock festival attired in a mini-miniskirt may suffice. The movement has its uniforms, rituals, and badges of membership. Older people sometimes put on the uniform in order to demonstrate that they are not entirely out of sympathy with the ideas and ideals of youth. Others, who are not without sympathy, refuse the beard and the beads simply because they detest all uniforms, whether worn by pigs, fascists, or revolutionaries.

But the rebelliousness of youth does not confine itself to the symbolisms of dress, language, and coiffure. Rejection of religion as traditionally practiced has become commonplace. New faiths are emergent, as among the hippies, and have more in common with Zen than anything orthodox to Christianity. Paul Goodman sees the young as primarily religious. If so, theirs is the kind of faith that mirrors John Dewey's distinction between religion and the religious.[1]

Equally significant is the antiwar and prolove stance of our young rebels. When generalized to embrace a way of life, it runs contrary to most American traditions. We now see mass protests on a grand scale. Riots, marches, sit-ins, love-ins, and mass assemblies surpass anything in our history. When a war moratorium brings hundreds of thousands of persons into public arenas, it can truly be called a "happening." Adults are puzzled by it all, and somewhat frightened.

A Concept of Relevant Curriculum

Young people are particularly critical of established educational practice. A common charge is that education lacks relevance. Often this criticism harks back to some of the traditions of old progressives in education. Sometimes, the charge means that education has not allied itself with the goals of revolutionaries, or that it has allied itself with business, labor, and the military.

What can education do these days that would be relevant? *We suggest that the schools incorporate in their curriculum a study of an important social movement, rejection by youth, and that this study emphasize examining, testing, and appraising the major beliefs caught up in this movement.* To pander to the instincts or impulses of rebellion would have little or no educational effect. The over-30 adult who simply "eggs on" his activist students does his clientele no service. A black studies program that fosters black nationalism or separatism would be equally obnoxious. If this is what youths mean by relevance, their wishes cannot be served.

Students find it all too easy to spot contradictions in the beliefs of their elders, and to explain all such discrepancies as instances of hypocrisy. They are a good deal less proficient in spotting their own inconsistencies, and they are quite convinced of their own sincerity. We need the kind of educational relevance that would help and require young people to examine their most basic assumptions about the kind of world that exists, and how they propose to change the world from what it is into something preferable. Students who rebel not only against the establishment but also against logical analysis may not at first perceive the relevance of this kind of education.

In order to achieve this kind of relevance, teachers will have to familiarize themselves with the thought patterns of students—their attitudes, values, beliefs, and interests. This can be done. It helps just to listen carefully to what young people are saying. Sometimes teachers who listen do not bore deeply enough into the meaning of what has been heard. They learn much about the surface thought of students but little, if anything, about what students "really think."

If we look closely at what students today believe, four issues or propositions in social analysis and processes of social change seem to prevail within the movement. Taken together, these four issues suggest a rejection of the liberal-reformist tradition. Liberalism is anathema to our youthful rebels. Liberalism is a failure, they say. Liberals talk much and do little. Many of the young leaders resemble the romantics who supported totalitarian movements in prewar Germany and Italy. A seldom observed and reported fact is that the candidacy of George Wallace in 1968 received more support from people under than over 30 years of age. A realignment in American politics that would place radicals and conservatives in alliance against liberalism is not without prospect.

A major issue that divides radicals from liberals is to be found in attitudes toward "The System." Liberals tend to assume that the system can best be changed and improved by working within it. They may agree with radicals that much in the system requires fundamental and sweeping change, but they also believe that the system is basically sound in that it permits and values change when rationally determined and implemented. In contrast, the radical would work against the system from the outside. He wants no part of the system, which he views as rotten throughout.

Liberals who suggest that schools assist students to examine the system in order to determine whether it is as rotten as some claim it to be are regarded as advocates of a delaying action. Radicals tend to view analysis of this kind as a form of social paralysis. It is not clearly established how many of today's young can properly be classified as radicals. An increasing number do believe that social change must begin with a total rejection of the existing system. Drastic change is preferred to any attempt to patch the existing system.

A second assumption that divides young people from the mainstream of American liberalism is over the relationship of means to ends. Liberals tend toward the assumption that the achievement of democratic ends requires the use of democratic means. Every means is an end, and every end a means to some further end. The quality of any end we achieve cannot be separated from the quality of the means used to achieve it. In contrast, many of the young assume that our kind of society can be transformed into a more democratic system only as people dare to employ undemocratic methods. They see no inconsistency in advocacy of free speech and denial of such freedom to their opposition. Some liberals agree with radicals on the need for drastic changes in the system, but they are unwilling to achieve such change except through processes of reason and persuasion.

A third assumption expresses on the part of the young a preference for intuitive and involved thinking as opposed to rational and detached thought. Many of the hippies, for example, have voiced a distaste for the logic and rationality of middle-class Americans. In contrast, liberals have criticized middle-class Americans for not being rational enough.

A part of the issue here is over the nature of rationality. Liberals do not agree that rational thought is necessarily detached or without involvement. Thought springs from the ground of social perplexity and concern. Objectivity is not the same as neutrality. Objectivity is a means by which to express concern and achieve conclusions. It is not to be used as a method by which to avoid conclusions or commitments. In the hands of some liberals, however, it has appeared to be a method by which to avoid rather than make value judgments. When they perceive objectivity as avoidance, concerned youth will look elsewhere for their philosophy. An intuition or existential leap may be their solution to any confusion that inhabits their minds. The popularity of the drug experience as a source of awareness and insight is consistent with this preference for intuitive methods of problem solving. The growing interest in parapsychology, extrasensory perception, spiritualism, and various versions of the occult manifests the same tendency to retreat from the use of reason in the study of social affairs.

A fourth assumption, issue, or proposition is over the nature, worth, and necessity of violence. The liberal eschews violence except when an organized minority thwarts the will of the majority, if that will seems to be the outcome of free discussion and reflective study of alternatives. The young, on the other hand, often regard reason and discussion as forms of compromise. It is quite defensible to take the law into one's hands if the law is unjust. One does not obey an unjust law until one is able to persuade others of its injustice and thus get it changed. Evasion of the law or open refusal to obey the law is an acceptable form of social protest, if personal conscience so dictates.

Basic to this issue is the question of whether or not drastic system change can be achieved without use of violence. Advocates of violence have not always distinguished between impressionistic and instrumental violence.[2] Impressionistic violence is the kind of hot response that results from deep-seated frustration over existing social conditions. Instrumental violence is more disciplined in nature and is followed deliberately and coolly as a method of social protest with social change as its objective.

The above four assumptions are basic in varying degree to the life outlook of young people who are in rebellion against established traditions. None of them is entirely new. Each has been tried and tested in a variety of social circumstances. Relevant history would reveal where such assumptions lead when acted upon under certain conditions. Yet none of these assumptions is today subjected to open, careful, and fair appraisal by a majority of schools or teachers. A relevant curriculum would take these assumptions seriously enough to make their study a major purpose of general education. Such study would help young people to understand their important personal problems, but would also open up for serious study the large social problems of our time.

Utopias, Relevant and Irrelevant[3]

A curriculum that would assist young people in an examination of their basic assumptions about society and its improvement must deal with values and social policies. Yet attention to values and social policies is now almost totally foreign to public schools.

Young people today will be in the prime of life by the year 2000. They can begin to think now about what they want as a society by that time. Four questions are basic to a curriculum that would start now to build toward future planning: 1) What kind of society now exists, and what are the dominant trends within it? 2) What kind of society is likely to emerge in the near future, let us say by the year 2000, if present trends continue? 3) What kind of society is preferable, given one's values? 4) If the likely and prognosticated society is different from the society that one prefers, what can the individual, alone or as a member of groups, do toward eliminating the discrepancy between prognostication and preference, between expectation and desire?

These questions are relevant to anyone, but they are particularly relevant to those young people who think in utopias and who agree with Buckminster Fuller that we now have to choose between utopia and oblivion.

We define utopia as any description of a society radically different from the existing one. Some utopias, as described, are relevant. Others are irrelevant. A relevant utopia is a model of a reformed world which not only spells out in specific and precise behavioral detail the contents of that new world but, in addition, provides a behavioral description of the transition to be made from the present system to the utopian one. Irrelevant utopias omit all solutions to the problem of transition. They may be precisely defined in behavioral terms, as in Butler's Erewhon, but provide no suggestions as to how one gets from where he is to where he wants to be.

Most utopias stated or implied by today's youth are irrelevant. Youth are fairly clear as to what they oppose. They desire a drastically different kind of social system, but they are not clear in any detailed sense as to what they desire as a system, or how that undefined system might be brought into being. To be relevant, youth, with encouragement from the schools, will have to engage in the kind of hard thinking that results in construction of social models. Hard thinking and model building are not always prized by youth who rely upon intuition and hunches for solutions to problems. Intuition is good enough for stating irrelevant utopias. It will not work, however, for those who value precisely stated concepts and tested solutions to the problem of social transition.

The search for relevant utopias should have great appeal to those youth who feel or believe that a drastic change in the social system is required for solution of today's problems. Its appeal lies in the fact that the search for relevance requires one to take seriously, and not merely romantically, the problem of how best to achieve drastic system change. Since drastic system change has occurred in the past, some study of a certain kind of history—not the kind usually taught in the schools—should be relevant to this search.

Relevant Utopias, Preferred Worlds

We have defined as a relevant utopia any social vision or dream that has been expressed as a social model with due regard for problems of precise definition and successful transition. From studies of existing society, numerous relevant utopias have been stated. In the area of international systems alone no less than nine models have been identified by Falk and Mendlovitz.[4] Each model may be used descriptively, predictively, and prescriptively. That is, each may be seen as a report of what already exists, as a prediction of what will soon exist, or as a prescription for what ought to exist in the near future. (Obviously, a model used only for descriptive purposes does not function as any kind of utopia, relevant or irrelevant. A person who sees the present international system in certain terms can encounter in another person a different description. Both persons may agree or disagree as to what they conceive utopia to be.) Much of the literature fails to make a clear distinction between descriptive and other uses of a model. The methodology of relevant utopias requires that such distinctions be consciously made. This methodology also requires us to take seriously any utopia that qualifies as relevant. But to take it seriously does not force us to prefer it.

One chooses his preferred world from the set of relevant utopias available to him. It is in the region of preferred worlds that individuality as prized by young radicals has a chance to express itself. A person who chooses his preferred world from a set of available relevant utopias must decide what risks he is prepared to take, and, obviously, persons differ greatly as to what risks they perceive and what risks they are willing to take.

An illustration from international relations and systems may serve to clarify this point. Grenville Clark and Louis Sohn have developed a relevant utopia that takes the form of limited world government. Their model consists of detailed amendments to the UN Charter which would give to the United Nations sufficient authority to prevent war, but without authority to intervene in the domestic affairs of nation-states. Another model, developed by Robert Hutchins and his colleagues at the University of Chicago, envisages a much more sweeping kind of world authority. The relationship within their model between the world authority and the nation-states resembles that which holds within the American federal system between the national government and the several states.

If one's choice is limited to these two models, which one should become one's preferred world? One can imagine a person who would say to himself: "The federal model is superior to the modified UN model for purposes of war prevention because it can get at the causes of war by intervening in the domestic affairs of nation-states. But the likelihood that any such world authority will come into being by the year 2000 is very dim. Yet some kind of world government is necessary if we are to have any chance of avoiding large-scale nuclear war. Therefore, I choose Clark-Sohn as my preferred world." Someone else might argue as follows: "Without an effective world government, nuclear disaster is bound to occur. Clark-Sohn, although feasible by the year 2000, could not possibly work. Hutchins, though very difficult to achieve, is my preferred world. To work for anything less would be a waste of time. I'll risk everything on reaching for the impossible. Perhaps my preference can even have some influence on the possibilities in the case."

Students have every right to differ with one another and with their teachers in their preferred worlds. They may also disagree as to whether a given utopia has been stated relevantly, as we have defined relevance. They may even disagree as to whether a particular utopia would be either effective, if adopted, or achievable, if pursued with zeal and rationality. They may also disagree as to whether utopian solutions are as necessary as some social critics claim. But these various differences are not always qualitatively the same. Whether a given model would work, or whether a given model is achievable in the near future, are factual questions; such questions can be answered only by ascertaining as rationally as possible what the probable facts are. But a difference in opinion over preferred worlds is not always a factual difference. It may be a difference involving values, preferred risks, life styles, and even personal temperament. One may use logic and evidence in choosing his preferred world, but logical men in possession of all the facts may not always agree on the world they prefer.

Personal Dilemmas, Social Concerns

A relevant curriculum is sometimes defined as one addressed to the personal problems of youth. This is not good enough. *It is more relevant to engage young people in a study of the problems of the larger culture in which many of their personal problems have their origin. The culture of most significance to the young consists of those aspects that are problematic—that is, the large conflicts and confusions which translate into the conflicts and confusions of individuals.*

To take one example, young people who are opposed to the war in Vietnam are reluctant to take a position against all war because the larger culture from which most of their learning continues to come expresses the same reluctance. In fact, many of the young insist upon the right to be conscientiously opposed to the war in Vietnam without a requirement that, out of conscience, they oppose all war. When asked the four questions basic to the methodology of relevant utopias as applied to the Vietnamese (What is Vietnam like today? What will it be like in the near future if present trends are extrapolated? What would you like it to be? What can you do about any discrepancy between extrapolation and values?), they are prone to reply that the fate of the Vietnamese is of no concern to them and that America should mind its own business. Their vaunted idealism is thus victimized by the widespread cultural preference for some form of isolationism. Although they do not like Nixon, they find it difficult to oppose his attempts to turn over the war to the Vietnamese. The methodology of relevant utopias would ask them to consider carefully whether or not Nixon's policies and their own view of those policies are at all adequate as steps transitional to a drastic change in the existing system of international relations. Unless they make an assessment of this kind, their opinions on a number of related personal and social matters are bound to reflect a great deal of confusion. They could end up as confused as the parents and grandparents whose views they reject.

Finally, what has been said about the use of relevant utopias in social analysis and prescription also applies to personal development and self-analysis. The significant questions are: What kind of person am I now? What kind will I become if present habits and trends persist? What kind of person would I like to become? What can be done now about tendencies and preferences that conflict? This approach to the problem of identity is more promising than some of the programs offered these days in the name of black studies, black history, and black pride. Historical and cultural studies have maximal relevance when they help us to predict the future or to make transition.

Notes

1. John Dewey, *A Common Faith* (New Haven, Connecticut: Yale University Press, 1934).

2. Charles Hamilton is to be credited with this distinction, as developed in a speech at Wingspread in 1968.

3. We are indebted to Saul Mendlovits of the World Law Fund, also professor of international law, Rutgers University, for development of the concept of relevant utopias.

4. Richard Falk and Saul Mendlovits (eds.), *A Strategy of World Order* (New York: World Law Fund, 1966).

9. Political Power and the High School Curriculum

John S. Mann

Political power is of concern to curriculum workers in at least three related ways. First, the effort to influence curriculum decisions is an exercise in political power. Such decisions are made, not on the basis of direct inference from definitive scholarly findings, but rather on the basis of a complex interaction of forces representing different interests, values, beliefs, and knowledge systems.

Second, since political power is a ubiquitous fact of societal existence, and since a democracy depends for its vigor and justness upon equitable distribution of power, it is proper that the citizens' schools offer extensive opportunities for learning about how political power operates.

Third, there are growing numbers of students who find our schools oppressive, inane, misconceived, and mismanaged, and who consequently are interested and involved in developing the political power they require to bring about very substantial improvements. Their efforts are increasingly a dominant component of the high school

Reprinted from *Educational Leadership* 28 (October 1970), 23-26. with permission of the Association for Supervision and Curriculum Development and the author. Copyright 1970 by the Association for Supervision and Curriculum Development.

environment, and thus willy-nilly have become an important "un-planned" part of the curriculum.

I will here try to describe one way of interpreting these three concerns in relation to one another and then briefly mention an approach to exploiting the potential in this regard. My approach is not eclectic. It reflects very strong partisan commitments about curriculum and politics. I shall try to make these commitments quite clear.

Dissident Views

I will begin with the dissident student and his dissatisfactions. He seems to the outsider to be in protest against everything established, and to see everything he opposes as essentially similar to everything else he opposes. Opposition to the draft, it would seem, is essentially the same thing as opposition to a silly dress code or an inadequate curriculum.

The rebellious student experiences each of these as immediate and direct oppression. And ending the war in Vietnam by expanding it into Cambodia and Laos reflects the same mentality that is involved in educating students to live in a democracy by denying them the most fundamental, as well as the most trivial, rights accorded citizens by our Constitution. From the students' point of view, education is not participation in a rigged and manipulated so-called "teaching-learning process," but rather a natural human consequence of and exercise in the uses of freedom. Our curriculum is manipulatory, mechanical, and inhuman, they assert, in precisely the same way that our approach to the problems of Indochina is manipulatory, mechanical, and inhuman.

A fundamental difference in world view is reflected here, and it is by virtue of this difference that the various protests blend into one. But this blending ought not to obscure what I believe is a matter of fact: that the center of gravity of student protest is nausea and rage over the way they are treated in school in the name of education. Nor is this fact mitigated by another equally apparent fact: that what passes for education is a consequence of very much the same forces as what passes for foreign policy. Protesting students are engaged in a struggle against many forms of oppression, but they are willing to put a good deal of their considerable energy and talent to work in the struggle against the oppression most immediate to their own experience, and that is the oppression of schooling.

Exploring Uses of Freedom

One way for me to make my partisanship in these matters clear is to state that I find this student view essentially correct. From it I draw certain conclusions which establish the relation of the third concern of the curriculum worker to the other two that I have mentioned.

The first conclusion I draw is this: the most pressing task before the contemporary curriculum worker is to revitalize the exploration of the uses of freedom in education. In the late 1930's some real progress was being made on the problem of rigorously operationalizing the progressive conceptions of interest, choice, and learner-centered structuring of educational programs. In the intervening three decades we have lost what little art we were beginning to have in this difficult task, and we are now back to debates at the very crude level of structured versus nonstructured educational programs. We must rediscover and expand our grasp of the art of building educative programs around the act of choosing.

One of the recurrent problems we have with this notion of choosing derives from the fact that many of its interpreters have been rooted in a highly individualistic liberal tradition which did not adequately handle the problem of interests or rights in conflict. The classroom behavior which reflects this inadequacy and which for many teachers defines the limiting factor in their ability to handle "choice" is the statement I have heard so often: "But if I let *you* do that, *everyone* will want to do it."

Choice in the context of school, like choice in the context of a broader democratic society, cannot entirely be a matter of each individual's doing his thing. Choices of individuals interact in very complex ways with choices of collectivities; such choices are a social and a political as well as an individual process, and bear upon both the conduct of life in school and the conduct of life in society. The second conclusion I draw, then, is that both the practice and the study of the social-political process of the exercise of choice is a crucial part of the educative experience. And, as I have argued in another paper,[1] choice is power in motion.

A Massive Political Effort

There are curriculum specialists who, steeped in the "progressive" conception of education, will be in basic agreement with my views both of the centrality of choice in a sound pedagogy and of the close interaction between social-political and educative processes. Yet they and I too often have been content to substitute vacuous rhetoric about "humanizing education" for action; and, when we have acted, too often the action has been a futile sort of patchwork affair, piecing little tidbits of humanism onto a thoroughly manipulative, impersonal, mechanical sort of curriculum.

We have had, it seems to me, a naïve belief that, if we would only display our humanism often enough, everyone would buy it. The third conclusion I draw is that reconstruction of our nation's schools along pedagogically progressive and politically democratic lines requires a massive and strident political effort.

These three conclusions establish the relations among the three concerns with which I began. Students are demanding drastic revision of both political and educational outlook and behavior. Their vision of the process by which education is to proceed is a synecdoche for their vision of the political process, so that the exercise of one is both a part of and a preparation for the other. And the current efforts among students to organize themselves into a coherent political force have the potential for drastically altering the balance of powers that now shapes school policy.

Alliance with Students

Given this outlook, the widespread tendency to respond to student movements with repressive measures appears to be either folly or malice. The dissident students have fundamental commitments in common with many of us who are professional educators; this includes professors, teachers, and curriculum and administrative personnel. They offer us the most viable course to fulfilling our commitment that has come along in many years. That course in its simple essence is alliance with them in a struggle against those individuals and institutions that stand for oppressive "educative" practices we have come to recognize as dehumanizing. The form the struggle is to take is an open question. It is quite clear that the students have made errors in analyzing educational issues. It is also clear that we have been irresponsible in failing to think seriously about political tactics at all and in failing to lend our skill to their analytic efforts.

Yet if one believes, as I do, that the thrust of their protest is both right and urgent, then the proper course of action would seem to be to support and strengthen their movement—to help make it a better movement.

There are at least three kinds of activity that the typical idealistic young radical is involved in that could be substantially supported by teachers and curriculum workers. First, he is engaged in criticizing and analyzing current school practices and formulating alternatives to these practices. Second, he is involved in learning (a) about his own political and legal powers and rights, (b) about the distribution of and legal constraints upon power in and around his school system, and (c) about other powers, such as groupings of teachers within the teachers union, with which a convergence of interests might lead to joining forces. Third, the dissident student is engaged in direct political action over specific issues, some of which are educational and some of which are more broadly political. Action here includes such things as leafleting, holding public meetings, soliciting support from other groups, picketing, parading—all the legal things that constitute participation in the democratic political process.

Mutual Benefit

In each of these three activities the dissident student has much to gain from the support and assistance of professional educators. And the professional educator who shares the commitments I have expressed in this paper also has much to gain. For in the restlessness of these highly committed and strongly motivated students he has an unprecedented opportunity simultaneously to build a prototypically progressive educational program, to cultivate the kind of understanding of political power that is required of citizens in a democracy, and to contribute to the growth and internal education of a political movement in opposition to current school practices that he finds destructive, oppressive, and as thoroughly misguided as they are firmly entrenched.

What I envision, but what I cannot spell out here in detail, is a movement to design a progressive curriculum specifically for these

angry radical students, in which thorough study of educational policy formulation and of the politics of schools would converge and be
reinforced, corrected, refined, and deepened in the practical experience of actually formulating educational policy and struggling to
enact it. It would make perfect sense, I think, for this experience
itself to constitute the major portion of the dissident student's curriculum for a semester or two in his junior or senior year.

This sort of curricular innovation will not be widely accepted by
school systems because it expresses a genuinely oppositional point of
view.[2] Its pedagogy, its political strategy, and its underlying assumptions diverge markedly from those of current school practices. I believe, though, that such an innovation provides a point of departure
for curriculum planning which is responsive to the interests and
world views of many high school students.

This approach will strike a responsive chord, too, in a large number of teachers who entered the profession with ideals they have long
since learned out of necessity to keep buried away.

We can do much more than merely talk about ways to "humanize
education." We can help the students with the kind of curriculum I
have hinted at in spite of opposition, which may mean doing it
before, after, and around instead of in school. We can seek out and
bring together like-minded teachers and cultivate support in related
professional and paraprofessional groupings. We can seek proper
bases for coalitions between our professional groups and dissident
student groups. We can become more aware, ourselves, of our own
historical roots and of the deep interlocks between current school
practice and other aspects of our national life.

These are some of the things educators can do to move beyond the
rhetoric of "humanizing education." I would expect that the progressive paradigm is as good for us as it is for the students. If so, then our
efforts to understand the relations between education and freedom
will themselves be refreshed, corrected, and deepened as we move
into a more direct and more active expression of our beliefs and
commitments.

Notes

1. John S. Mann, "The Curriculum Worker: A View of His Training and His
Tasks," *Educational Comment 1970* (Toledo: University of Toledo, 1970).

2. Remember the point Charles Beard, among others, has made, that in a democratic society schools must be left free to criticize the society that sponsors them. The same relation obtains between a particular program and a school system that sponsors it. See Charles Beard, *The Unique Function of Education in American Democracy* (Washington, D.C.: National Education Association, 1937).

10. The Rediscovery of Purpose in Education

Harold G. Shane

Something seemed to go awry with the once-sustaining purposes of U.S. education in the years between 1920 and 1970. By the late 1960's there was even the gloomy prospect that our instructional landscape might be on the way to becoming a littered ideological junkyard.

As we entered the 1970's there undoubtedly were more than a few Americans who uneasily speculated, and not without some reason, that we were moving into a confused, "Twilight of the Goals" interval which foreshadowed a social and educational Armageddon that was likely to occur in the next decade or two.

The Rediscovery of Basic Purpose

Because of contemporary educational problems too well known to need recounting, it is suggested here with a sense of urgency that the need for a rediscovery of educational purpose is becoming frighten-

Reprinted from *Educational Leadership* 28 (December 1970), 245-49, with permission of the Association for Supervision and Curriculum Development and the author. Copyright 1971 by the Association for Supervision and Curriculum Development.

ingly obvious. After 10,000 years we appear to have come full circle and once again need to rediscover the purpose of primitive man's education—human survival in the face of a dangerous, implacable environment.

From a life-and-death battle with a hostile nature early in our history we have cycled back to a point at which we face an analogous struggle to protect ourselves from an environment—a biosphere, to use fashionable terminology—which has been made dangerous *for* man *by* man. Among the present, clear dangers are our propensity for overbreeding, our ingenuity in devising deadly weapons, the careless release of poisonous technological wastes, and the thoughtlessly accumulated mountains of "indisposable" trash which crowd our living space.

It is simple to propose that learning to survive has become a new central goal of education; it is decidedly less simple to conjecture about how to go about approaching such an objective.

Attaining New "Survival Behaviors"

At least two paths of action present themselves if we accept the concept that survival in a meaningful world is an immediate goal for education. One of these is a reinterpretation of what constitutes "survival behaviors." The other is an educational reformation which will not only permit but which will begin to ensure that children and youth in our schools put together valid "behavioral survival kits." Such kits will help them not only to make it into the next century but, in the process, to begin to recast the world so that it promises to remain a nutritive bioenvironment suitable for mankind to inhabit. Let us look first at survival behavior.

From earliest times the notion of survival was associated with attaining and staying at the apex of a socioeconomic pyramid. At least until the nineteenth century, about 15 percent of Western Europe's population—aristocrats, soldiers, ecclesiastics, scholars—was supported by the laborers, agrarians, and artisans making up the other 85 percent. Man fought like Duke William at Hastings to get to the top of the pile and schemed like King John at Runnymede to stay there. Indeed, through the ages, history has defined the one who survives as "successful" and has bestowed its worldly favors on those caesars who proved to have the highest "survival quotients" in life's arenas!

In the past century, however, science, technology, and democracy have combined to invert the human pyramid. Today in the United States, no more than 7 percent of the population is needed on our mechanized farms to produce food for the remaining 93 percent. Theoretically, one-third of our adults, by 1985, would not even need to be productive workers. The remaining two-thirds of the U.S. population doubtless could meet not only their own material needs but those of tens of millions of others who would produce nothing. This is a projection of a repugnant possibility, however, and not a prophecy!

Despite the reversal of our human pyramid, a 50,000-year interval of deep-rooted survival behavior is not quickly forgotten. For the most part, society and its schools have both failed to teach and failed to understand that man is becoming more capable of surviving by living with his fellows rather than by living on his fellows. Conjecture clearly suggests that there is not only "room at the top" but room everywhere for self-realization and for a better life for all in the inverted social pyramid of the present century if we can discipline ourselves to make the needed "survival decisions." To put it bluntly, a 180° reversal is needed in the traditional concept of "get-ahead behavior" that man has learned to accept during the past 500 centuries. We now need to learn how to stop behaving like troglodytes in trousers and take the steps that lead from being the scattered members of insecure tribes to becoming a secure mankind.

New Purpose as a Source of Direction for Educational Change

Educational reforms of a sweeping and significant nature rarely have come about through the action of the schools in and of themselves. Educational practice tends to reflect what a majority or at least a plurality of society chooses to support in the classroom. Under such circumstances it seems reasonable to argue that society itself must make itself accountable for changes that are needed in the fabric of teaching and learning in order to bring us closer to a new central purpose for education.

Below is a sample of the kind of neglected or minimized learnings that a society interested in the survival and in the physical and psychological health of the children and youth should mandate that its schools recognize:

(1) That we need to begin to lead less wasteful, extravagant lives, to do with less, and to rediscover enjoyment in simpler activities, objects, and pleasures so that our posterity will not live a marginal existence in a world stripped half naked of its inheritance;

(2) That the despoliation of our forests and the pillage of our pure air and clean water shall cease along with the poorly managed exploitation of fuels, fertile soils, and metals. Such abuses must be terminated by group consensus and by the legislation to which it leads;

(3) That no one has the right to befoul or poison the earth with chemicals or radioactive wastes or poorly removed sewage and garbage;

(4) That unless we exercise prudence and personal responsibility, we will suffer badly from the malignant consequences of changes that affect man's relationships with his environment, as in faulty city planning, random dam building, or unwise land use;

(5) That there is a need to understand the immediate danger of irresponsible and uncontrolled human breeding as the world's population builds up toward the 4 billion mark;

(6) That the folly of conflict is becoming more and more incongruous in a world grown capable of self-destruction;

(7) That mass media need to become more positive agents for reinforcing the educational guidance of the young, for producing less misleading advertising, for more thoughtful and less strident news, and for a more accurate and dignified portrayal of life in the global village;

(8) That we must learn to be more personally responsible for the participation and earned support that are needed to ensure an increase in the number of able, dedicated public servants in elective and appointive governmental offices.

The Deeper Meaning of "Relevance"

What we mean by relevance in education is implicit in the previous eight points. Relevance is more than teaching subject matter and providing experiences that the young say they find immediately meaningful, more interesting, and more useful to them. A relevant education, an education for survival, is one which introduces children and youth to participation in the tasks that they and adults confront together in the real world of the 1970's.

Furthermore, if we are to make rapid progress toward the successful attainment of a new central purpose for education, society must not only encourage but require that the schools work to produce a generation of hardheaded young people committed to survival yet remembering the meaning of compassion; persons who have been taught the *Realpolitik* of life with honesty but who are nonetheless untainted by cynicism because they believe that it is not yet too late to cope with man's threat to himself.

The First Step in Reformation

Making a beginning in reform is not up to "society" as an abstract entity but to each of us as the individuals who make up society. It is through a new sense of imprescriptible personal responsibility that we can dispel the threatening twilight that recently has shadowed our goals.

In the process of creating a more benign environment, some of our sensate pleasures and much of our conspicuous consumption must diminish. Also, today's thoughtless waste of human and material resources must first be decreased and then ended as quickly as possible. In the process our lives will perforce become not only simpler and less hedonistic; they will become more people-centered and less thing-centered. This necessary redirection can bring us far more gain than loss. The satisfactions of 40 or 50 years ago were not necessarily less warm or less desirable because feet, bicycles, or street cars transported an older generation to shops, schools, or the theaters!

Furthermore, the short- and long-range changes that an endangered world requires for its future well-being should also involve fewer tensions, less erosive competition, and a clearer, more relaxing perspective with regard to what is most worth doing and most worth having.

A Concluding Conjecture

Assuming we do avoid extinction, there would seem to be two levels or kinds of survival for man: as a biological species and as humans. The eight survival learnings itemized here should help to ensure that the species is around for some time to come. If nothing else, sheer panic seems likely soon to motivate us to diminish the interrelated problems of ecology, of hunger, of waste, and of conflict.

To survive in a truly human context rather than a merely biological one is something else! Here we come to a more subtle aspect of a "survival kit" for young learners. Our rediscovery of purpose and of personal responsibility for the social and educational reforms that are prerequisite to physical survival is but one side of the coin.

There is the concomitant task of helping the young of each generation to discover for themselves a moral, aesthetic, intellectual, and scientific heritage that they see cause for making a part of themselves. Does it not then seem reasonable that our success in guiding this freshening, continuing rediscovery by the young of what makes us human is what gives the real meaning to "education for survival"?

And may one not rightly conjecture that, as a society of the individually responsible accepts this task, it simultaneously could become its own best hope for survival through the rediscovery of sustaining purpose in education?

Selected References for Social Reconstructionism-Relevance

Boulding, Kenneth. "Education for the Spaceship Earth," *Social Education* 32 (November 1968), 648-52.

Brameld, Theodore. "A Cross-cutting Approach to the Curriculum: The Moving Wheel," *Phi Delta Kappan* 51 (March 1970), 346-48.

Cloak, F. T., Jr. "Reach out or Die out," *Educational Leadership* 26 (April 1969), 661-65.

Davis, O. L., Jr. "Understanding Technology and Media: A Curriculum Imperative," *Educational Leadership* 26 (October 1968), 65-71.

Freire, Paulo. "The Adult Literacy Process as Cultural Action for Freedom," *Harvard Educational Review* 40 (May 1970), 205-225; and *Pedagogy of the Oppressed* (New York: Herder and Herder, 1970).

Guerney, Bernard, Jr., and M. L. Merriam. "Toward a Democratic Elementary-School Classroom," *Elementary School Journal* 72 (April 1972), 372-83.

Hartwell, A. S. "A Curriculum Design for Social Change," *Educational Leadership* 25 (Fall 1968), 405-407.

Illich, Ivan. *De-Schooling Society* (New York: Harper and Row, 1971).

Part Five
Curriculum as Academic Rationalism

The major goal of academic rationalists as far as curriculum is concerned is to enable students to use and appreciate the ideas and works that constitute the various intellectual and artistic disciplines. Academic rationalists argue that ideas within the various disciplines have a distinctive structure and a distinctive set of contributions to make to the education of man. Indeed, acquisition of these structures is largely what education is about.

Joseph Schwab's article presents a coherent and lucid introduction to the meaning of the structure of the disciplines. The last chapter, excerpted from a larger work by Hirst and Peters, presents a modification of the more classical academic-rationalistic position by arguing for a rationale for curriculum that emphasizes not topics or subjects but forms of thought. It is these forms of thought that provide the basis for curricula that aspire toward educational ends.

11. The Concept of the Structure
of a Discipline

Joseph J. Schwab

In 1941, my colleagues and I offered for the first time a course in
the structure of the disciplines. We had devoted an entire year to
developing its plan and content. But we had spent no time at all on
the problem of how to teach it. The first few weeks, in consequence,
were a severe trial of our students' patience. Finally, one of them
cornered me.

"Tell me," she said, "what this course is about."

I did so—in twelve minutes. I was impressed by my clarity as much
as by my brevity. So, apparently, was my student. For she eyed me a
moment and then said, "Thank you. Now I understand. And if the
truth is that complicated, I am not interested."

The young lady was right on two of three counts. First, the concept of a structure of a discipline is concerned in a highly important
sense with truth, not with truth in some vaguely poetic sense, but
with answerable, material questions of the extent to which, and the
sense in which, the content of a discipline is warranted and meaningful. Second, study of the structures of the disciplines is complicated
—at least by contrast to the simple assumptions about truth and

Reprinted from *The Educational Record* 43 (July 1962), 197-205, with permission of the author and the publisher, the American Council on Education.

meaning which we have used in the past in determining the content and the organization of the school curriculum.

On the third count, however, the young lady was wrong. We cannot afford to be uninterested in the structures of the disciplines. We cannot so afford because they pose problems with which we in education must deal. The structures of the modern disciplines are complex and diverse. Only occasionally do we now find among them a highly esteemed body of knowledge which consists simply of collections of literal statements standing in one-for-one relation to corresponding facts. Instead of collections, we find organizations in which each member statement depends on the others for its meaning. And the verifying relations of such organizations to their facts are convoluted and diverse. This complexity of modern structures means that problems of comprehension and understanding of modern knowledge now exist which we in education have barely recognized. The diversity of modern structures means that we must look, not for a simple theory of learning leading to a one best learning-teaching structure for our schools, but for a complex theory leading to a number of different structures, each appropriate or "best" for a given discipline or group of disciplines.

In brief, the structures of the disciplines are twice important to education. First, they are necessary to teachers and educators: they must be taken into account as we plan curriculum and prepare our teaching materials; otherwise, our plans are likely to miscarry and our materials, to misteach. Second, they are necessary in some part and degree within the curriculum, as elements of what we teach. Otherwise, there will be failure of learning or gross mislearning by our students.

Let us turn now to examination of a structure, using the sciences as the example.

Forty years ago it was possible for many scientists and most educators to nurse the illusion that science was a matter of patiently seeking the facts of nature and accurately reporting them. The conclusions of science were supposed to be nothing more than summaries of these facts.

This *was* an illusion, and it was revealed as such by events in the science of physics that began in the late 1890's. The discovery of radioactivity suddenly revealed a world within the world then thought to be the only world. The study of that world and of its relations to the world already known led to a revolution in the goals and the structures of physics. By the mid-twenties, this revolution in physics had gone so far that we were faced with the fact that some of the oldest and least questioned of our ideas could no longer be treated as literally true—or literally false. Classical space had been a homogeneous, neutral stage on which the dramas of motion and existence were acted out. The flow of classical time was always and everywhere the same. The mass and length of bodies were each elementary properties independent of other properties. Bodies occupied a definite location and a definite amount of space.

The new physics changed these notions. In its knowledge structure, space was something which could be distorted, and its distortions affected bodies in it. The magnitude and position of subatomic particles could not be described as we describe the magnitude and position of a one-inch cube here-now.

But these new assertions did *not* come about because direct observations of space, place, time, and magnitude disclosed that our past views about them were merely mistaken. Rather, our old assertions about these matters were changed because physicists had found it fruitful to treat them in a new way—neither as self-evident truths nor as matters for immediate empirical verification. They were to be treated, instead, as principles of inquiry—conceptual structures which could be revised when necessary, in directions dictated by large complexes of theory, diverse bodies of data, and numerous criteria of progress in science.

Today, almost all parts of the subject-matter sciences proceed in this way. A fresh line of scientific research has its origin not in objective facts alone, but in a conception, a deliberate construction of the mind. On this conception, all else depends. It tells us what facts to look for in the research. It tells us what meaning to assign these facts.

A moment's thought is enough to show us how this process operates. That we propose to investigate a chosen subject is to say, of course, that we are, in large part, ignorant of it. We may have some knowledge, based on common experience or on data garnered in preliminary study. But this preliminary knowledge is only a nibbling at the edges. We barely know the superficial exterior of our subject, much less its inner character. Hence, we do not know with certainty what further facts to look for, what facts will tell us the significant story of the subject in hand. We can only guess.

In physiology, for example, we did not know, but only supposed, that the functioning of the human organism is carried out by distinct parts, that each part has a character and a fixed function in the economy of the whole. Hence, we did not know that the facts we ought to seek in physiological research should be facts about the structure of each organ and what happens when each organ is removed. On the contrary, the conceptions of organ and of function were developed prior to sure knowledge of these matters and were developed precisely to make such knowledge possible through research. The conceptions are guiding principles of inquiry, not its immediate fruits.

In physics, similarly, we did not know from the beginning that the properties of particles of matter are fundamental and determine the behavior of these particles, their relations to one another. It was not verified knowledge but a heuristic principle, needed to structure inquiry, that led us to investigate mass and charge and, later, spin.

It may, indeed, be the case that the particles of matter are social particles, that their most significant properties are not properties of their very own but properties which accrue to them from association with other particles, properties that change as the associations change. Therefore, it may be that the more significant facts to seek in physical inquiry are not facts about the properties of particles but facts about kinds of associations and the consequences of associations.

Similar alternatives exist for physiology. There are conceptions of the organism that yield, when pursued in inquiry, a more profound knowledge than that afforded by the notions of organ and function.

In short, what facts to seek in the long course of an inquiry and what meaning to assign them are decisions that are made before the fact. The scientific knowledge of any given time rests not on the facts but on selected facts—and the selection rests on the conceptual principles of the inquiry.

Moreover, scientific knowledge—the knowledge won through inquiry—is not knowledge merely of the facts. It is of the facts interpreted. This interpretation, too, depends on the conceptual principles of the inquiry. The structure-function physiologist does not report merely the numerous changes displayed by an experimental animal from which an organ has been removed. He interprets these changes as indicative of the lost function once performed by the organ removed. It is this interpretation of the facts that is the

— conclusion drawn from the experiment and reported as a piece of
scientific knowledge, and its meaning and validity depend on the
conception of organ and function as much as they depend on the
selected facts.

Here, then, is a first approximation of what is meant by the structure of a discipline. The structure of a discipline consists, in part, of
the body of imposed conceptions which define the investigated subject matter of that discipline and control its inquiries.

The significance to education of these guiding conceptions becomes clearer if we repeat once more the way in which they act as
guides. First, they severely restrict the range of data which the scientist seeks in inquiry. He does not study the whole of his subject, but
only some aspect of it, an aspect which his then-current principles of
inquiry lead him to treat as the significant aspect. The conclusions of
that line of inquiry may be true, but most certainly they are not the
whole truth about that subject matter. They are not about some
aspect of nature taken in its pristine state but about something which
the principles of the inquiry have made, altered, or restricted. Furthermore, what the scientist makes of these data, what he takes them
to mean, is also determined not by full knowledge of their significance, but by the tentative principles of the inquiry.

Now the subject matter may be—in fact, almost always is—far
richer and more complex than the limited model of it embodied in
the conclusions of the restricted inquiry. Thus, the first significance
to education of the structure of a discipline: we cannot, with im-
punity, teach the conclusions of a discipline as if they were about the
whole subject matter and were the whole truth about it. For the
intelligent student will discover in time—unless we have thoroughly
blinded him by our teaching—that any subject behaves in ways which
do not conform to what he has been told about it. His bodily ill-
nesses, for example, are often not reducible to the malfunctioning of
specific organs or the presence of a specific bacterium. His auto-
mobile does not appear to obey the "laws" of the particular science
of mechanics which he was taught. Legislatures and executives do
not behave as a dogmatic political science says they do.

It is the case, however, that a structure-function physiology, a
Newtonian mechanics, or some particular reading of political behavior throws *some* light on the behavior of our bodies, our automo-
biles, or our democracy. Or it would if the body of knowledge were

understood in the light of the restricted circumstances in which it is valid and known in connection with the restricted range of data which it subsumes. In short, the bodies of knowledge would have defensible and valuable meaning to those who learn them had they been learned, not in a context of dogma, but in a context of the conceptions and data that determine their limited meaning and confer their limited validity. This is one significance of the structure of the disciplines to education.

A second significance becomes visible if we look at a further consequence of the operation of a conceptual structure in inquiry. It renders scientific knowledge fragile and subject to change; research does not proceed indefinitely on the basis of the principles that guided its first inquiries. On the contrary, the same inquiries that accumulate limited knowledge by the aid of assumed principles of inquiry also test these principles. As the selected principles are used, two consequences ensue. Knowledge of the subject unfolds; experimental techniques are refined and invented. The new knowledge lets us envisage new, more adequate, more telling conceptions of the subject matter. The growth of technique permits us to put the new conceptions into practice as guiding principles of a renewed inquiry.

The effect of these perennial renewals of inquiry is perennial revision of scientific knowledge. With each change in conceptual system, the older knowledge gained through use of the older principles sinks into limbo. The facts embodied are salvaged, reordered, and reused, but the knowledge which formerly embodied these facts is replaced. There is, then, a continuing and pervasive revision of scientific knowledge as principles of inquiry are used, tested, and supplanted.

Furthermore, our scientific and scholarly establishment is now so large; so many men are now engaged in inquiry that the rate of this revision is exceedingly rapid. We can expect radical reorganization of a given body of scientific knowledge, not once in the coming century but several times, at intervals of five to fifteen years. This means, of course, that our students—if they continue to receive all their learning in a dogmatic context, outside the structure of the disciplines— will confront at least once in their lives what appears to be a flat contradiction of much that they were taught about some subject. The effect of this lie-direct to teachings of the schools can only be exacerbation, to an intolerable degree, of the confusion, uncertainty, and cynicism which our young people already exhibit with respect to expertise, to schooling, and to bodies of organized knowledge.

Our students and our nation could be protected from the consequences of such misunderstanding, if, again, our students learned what they learned not as a body of literal and irrevocable truths but as what it is: one embodiment of one attack on something less than the whole of the matter under investigation. This is a second significance of the conceptual structure of the disciplines to education.

Whereas the second significance to education arises from the existence of a process of revision, the third and fourth significances emerge from the outcomes of this process—from the advances which it has made possible. In the process of revision, improvement of principle is sought in two different directions. On the one hand, more valid principles are sought, principles which will embrace more and more of the richness and complexity of the subject under investigation. On the other hand, principles of wider scope are sought, principles which will embrace a wider and wider range of subject matters, which will reduce what were before considered as separate and different phenomena to related aspects of a common kind or source. (Thus, Newtonian mechanics united the movements of the heavenly bodies with the behavior of objects thrown and dropped by man on earth, rendering these formerly diverse phenomena but varying expressions of a common law. Similarly, the physics of the century just past found new principles that united the formerly separated phenomena of light, electricity, and magnetism.)

The successful search for more valid principles—for more adequate models of investigated phenomena—has led to scientific knowledge of a new "shape" or character, in sharp contrast to older knowledge. Older knowledge tended toward the shape of a catalogue. Old descriptive biology, for example, was necessarily a catalogue: of the organs, tissues, or kinds of cells which made up the body. Another part of descriptive biology was a catalogue of the species, genera, classes, and so on of the living organisms that populated the earth. Even the experimental physiology of years only recently past tended toward a similarly encyclopedic character—for example, lists of parts of bodies with their functions, meticulous itemizing of hereditary units and their consequent traits. Chemistry, in similar fashion, tended to be a classificatory scheme of elements and of the more complex substances that arose from their combination.

Modern scientific inquiry, conversely, tends to look for patterns—patterns of change and patterns of relations—as their explanatory principles. When such patterns are found, they throw a new and more complex light on the items of our old catalogues. The items lose their primary significance and lose their independence. On the side of significance, an item ceases to be something which simply is, and becomes, instead, one of possibly many "somethings" that fulfill conditions required by the pattern. On the side of dependence-independence, an item ceases to be something which can be understood by itself; it becomes, instead, something which can be understood only by knowing the relations it bears to the other items that fill out the pattern or blueprint.

Thus, it was once possible to teach something about the significance of glucose to the living body by reciting a formula for it—naming the three elements which compose it, indicating the number of each—and naming it as an energy source. Today, it is necessary to talk about the basic pattern of a carbohydrate molecule, how the elements are connected to one another, what happens when connections are made or broken, and so on. This story of pattern is imbedded, in turn, in a still larger pattern—the pattern of processes by which energy is captured, stored, transferred, and utilized in the body. The educational significance of this emphasis on pattern in the sciences is more clearly indicated by the further point that, a few years ago, we could tell the story of energy sources merely by cataloguing glucose and two or three other substances as the common energy sources of the body. Today, the story must be the story of where and when and under what circumstances each of these substances functions as an energy source, and how, in a sense, they function as interchangeable parts to fulfill the conditions of the determining pattern.

This shift from catalogues to patterns in the disciplines means, in turn, that teaching and learning take on a new dimension. Instead of focusing on one thing or idea at a time, clarifying each and going on to the next, teaching becomes a process of focusing on points of contact and connection among things and ideas, of clarifying the effect of each thing on the others, of conveying the way in which each connection modifies the participants in the connection—in brief, the task of portraying phenomena and ideas not as things in themselves but as fulfillments of a pattern.

The successful search for principles of greater scope has led to developments of a parallel kind. As the scope of a set of principles enlarges, so does the coherence of the body of knowledge which develops from it, the interdependence of its component statements, a fifth significance. Thus, in a theory which embraces electricity and magnetism as well as light, an assertion about the nature of light borrows part of its meaning and part of its warrant from statements about electricity and magnetism. The significance of the assertion about light cannot be grasped by understanding only its terms and the light phenomena to which it applies. For these terms are defined in part by terms in other statements about other phenomena.

This kind of coherence in scientific knowledge means that our most common way of applying the old query "What knowledge is of most worth?" is no longer entirely defensible. We can no longer safely select from the conclusions of the disciplines the separate and different bits and pieces that we think would be most useful to the clients of the schools. We cannot because the separation of these bits, their removal from the structure of other statements which confer on them their meaning, alters or curtails that meaning. The statements will no longer convey the warranted and valid knowledge they convey in context, but something else or something less.

For students of some ages or of very limited learning competence, such bits and pieces may be appropriate as limited guides to limited actions, limited understanding, and a limited role in society. For many children at many ages, however, we need to face the fact that such a disintegrated content is not only a distorted image of scientific knowledge but a distorted image of the physical world it purports to represent; it will betray itself.

This means, in turn, that teaching and learning, as we have suggested above, need an added dimension. As patterns replace lists and catalogues, learning and remembering of parts remain necessary conditions of learning, but cease to be sufficient conditions. A new flexibility is required, a capacity to deal with the roles of things, as well as with things as such, and to understand the relations among roles. The following crude metaphor may suggest the nature of this flexibility. Natural phenomena as now conceived by the sciences must be understood as a dynamic, a drama. The drama unfolds as the outcome of many interacting roles. Therefore, the relation of each role to others must be understood. Second, each role may be played by more than one actor; different "actors," despite their apparent diversities, must be recognized as potential players of the same role. Third, each potential player of a role modifies somewhat the role he plays and, through this effect, also modifies the roles played by other actors. Hence, the unfolding, the climax, and outcome of the drama are flexible, not one rigid pattern, but variations on a theme.

A sixth significance of conceptual principle to education is quickly told.

Different disciplines have widely different conceptual structures. Despite the passionate concern of some philosophers and some scientists for a unity of the sciences, biologists and physicists, for example, continue to ask widely different questions in their inquiries, seek different kinds of data, and formulate their respective bodies of knowledge in widely different forms. It is not quite obsolete in biology, for instance, to ask what system of classes will best organize our knowledge of living things and to seek data primarily in terms of similarities and differences. The physicist, however, continues to find it most rewarding to ask what relations among what varying quantities will best organize our knowledge of the behavior of matter; consequently, he seeks data which consist primarily of measurements of such changing quantities.

Such differences among sciences are so persistent and so rewarding that it is hard to avoid the conviction that there are real and genuine differences among different bodies of phenomena, that differences in questions put and data sought are not merely the products of historical habits among the different disciplines but also reflect some stubbornnesses of the subjects. Some subject matters answer when one set of questions is put. Another answers to another set. And neither will answer the questions to which the other responds.

Among these differences of conceptual structure, there are some which deserve special attention from educators because of the confusion they create if ignored. These are the specific differences among conceptions which two or more disciplines apparently hold in common. Two large-scale examples occur to me: the concept of time and the concept of class.

Time is deeply imbedded in the conceptual structure of both physics and biology. In many respects, the concept of time is the same in both sciences. In one respect it is radically different. Time for the biologist is unavoidably vectorial and has direction from past to future, like the time of common sense. It cannot, in any sense, be considered reversible. Time, as it appears in most physical equations, in contrast, has no notion of past and future attached to it; it permits, in a certain sense, reversibility.

The concept of class is, perhaps, a more telling instance of difference for the purposes of education. The class of biology is a loose and messy affair compared to the class with which traditional logic (and much of mathematics) is concerned. The logical class consists of members which are all alike in some defining respect. The biologists' class, however, consists of members of which it can be said, at best, that most of them have most of many properties which, together, define the class.

The special problem posed by such differences as these is easily seen. The logical class, consisting of members alike in some defining respect, permits us to infer with confidence knowledge about members of the class from knowledge of the class. The biological class permits no such confident inference. What is true for the class may or may not be true of some member or subclass. Obviously, instruction which permitted this crucially instrumental conceptual difference to go unnoted by teachers and students would lead to all sorts of later confusion and error.

I remarked earlier that a body of concepts—commitments about the nature of a subject matter, functioning as a guide to inquiry—was one component of the structure of a discipline. Let us turn briefly to another which I shall call the syntactical structure of the disciplines. By the syntax of a discipline, I mean the pattern of its procedure, its method, how it goes about using its conceptions to attain its goals.

Most of us were taught a schoolbook version of a syntax under the guise of "scientific method." Though oversimple, full of error, and by no means the universal method of the sciences, it will suffice as an example. This schoolbook story (borrowed, incidentally, from an early work of Dewey) tells us that science proceeds through four steps. There is, first, the noting of data relevant to our problem. Second, there is the conceiving of a hypothesis. Third, the hypothesis is tested by determining whether consequences expected if the hypothesis were true are, in fact, found to occur. Finally, a conclusion is stated, asserting the verification or nonverification of the hypothesis.

So we are given the impression that the goal of all the sciences is a congeries of well-verified hypotheses. We are left with the impression that verification is of only one kind—the discovery that expected consequences occur in fact.

If this were all there were to the syntax of the disciplines, it would be of little importance to teaching, learning, and the curriculum. Unfortunately, this is not all there is. For different disciplines have different starting points and different goals. That is, their subject matters may be conceived in vastly different ways, so also may what they conceive to be sound knowledge or fruits of the inquiry. Consequently, the path, the syntax, the process of discovery and verification is also different.

Such differences in method of verification and discovery hold even for the similar disciplines called the sciences. They hold, *a fortiori*, between the sciences on one count, mathematics on another, and history on a third.

Among the sciences, let us contrast, once more, biology and physics. Biology, until very recently, has been the science that comes closest to fulfilling the schoolbook version of science. It has consisted, in large part, of a congeries of tested hypotheses. Its inquiries have turned from the verification of one to the verification of another with little twinge of conscience. Biologists have rarely hesitated to formulate hypotheses for different problems that differed widely from one another, that had little, indeed, of a common body of conceptions. Thus, verification for biology was largely a matter of chasing down, one by one, many and various expected consequences of many and various hypotheses.

Physics, on the other hand, has for centuries held as its goal not a congeries of almost independent hypotheses but a coherent and closely knit body of knowledge. It has sought to impose on its diverse formulations of diverse phenomena a body of conceptions which would relate them to one another and make of them one body, inferable from the conceptions which bound them together. Hence, for physics, verification has often meant something far otherwise than its meaning in biology. It has meant, in many cases, that expected consequences had been observed. In a few cases, however, the first reason for accepting a certain hypothetical had nothing to do with observed consequences. Rather, the hypothetical in question was accepted in order to save another conception, one which lay deep in the structure of physical knowledge and had ramifications extending over most of its conclusion. Thus, the "verifying" circumstance had to do with the structure of existing knowledge rather than the structure of existing things. (In one such case, the hypothetical in question—the neutrino—was verified some years later by the discovery of expected consequences, to the great relief of many physicists. In still another case—that of the parity principle—the principle itself was discarded and replaced.)

Where physics and biology differ in their goals, science and mathematics differ primarily in their starting points, that is, their subject matters. The consequent differences in their syntax are vast. Let us take algebra as our example and agree for the moment that the subject matter of algebra is number. Now, whatever number may be, one thing is certain: it does not consist of a body of material things, of events accessible to our senses. The idea of testing for the presence of materially existential consequences is meaningless in algebra. The algebraist may conceivably use something called data, but, if he does, it is something vastly different from what is meant by data in a science which studies a material, sense-accessible subject matter. Yet, there can be error as well as truth in algebra, hence, some means of discovery and of test. Clearly, then, the means, the syntax of mathematics, must be vastly different from the syntax which has a material subject matter.

A similar great difference holds between most history and the sciences. Few historians would hold that their goal, like the goal of science, is discovery of general laws. They do not take as their starting points things and events which they think of as repeated instances of a kind of thing or event. On the contrary, most historians take as their goal the recovery or the reconstruction of some selected, time-limited or space-limited group of past and unique events. But again, there are such things as better history and worse history— the more and the less well verified. Yet, only by the wildest of equivocations can we assert that the historian discovers and verifies in the same way as does the investigator of living things, of falling bodies, or of numbers.

In brief, truth is a complicated matter. The conceptual structure of a discipline determines what we shall seek the truth about and in what terms that truth shall be couched. The syntactical structure of a discipline is concerned with the operations that distinguish the true, the verified, and the warranted in that discipline from the unverified and unwarranted. Both of these—the conceptual and the syntactical—are different in different disciplines. The significance for education of these diverse structures lies precisely in the extent to which we want to teach what is true and have it understood.

12. The Curriculum

P. H. Hirst and R. S. Peters

Introduction

The last two chapters have brought to the fore two of the logical demands that all adequately planned educational practice must face.[1] First, there is the inescapable matter of determining somehow the aims, ends, or objectives of the enterprise. Secondly, there is the crucial point that, if we examine carefully the character of the central objectives sought by progressives, we find that they, as much as those sought by traditionalists, are necessarily related to the acquisition of certain fundamental forms of what we have loosely called public modes of experience, understanding, and knowledge.

As has already been indicated, it is not the purpose of this book to pursue the first of these demands further. That education necessitates decisions of this kind is a philosophical point. The actual decisions themselves are, however, not properly made by attending to philosophical considerations only. Psychological, social, economic, and other factors are equally important. Yet the relevant philosophi-

Reprinted from P. H. Hirst and R. S. Peters, *The Logic of Education* (1970) with permission of the authors and the publisher, Routledge & Kegan Paul, Ltd., and Humanities Press, Inc.

cal considerations are precisely our concern, and the second demand that has emerged is of this kind. Its significance will, therefore, now be pursued further within the more specific context of curriculum planning.

Curriculum Objectives

(a) *The need for objectives.* We shall take the term *curriculum* to be the label for a program or course of activities which is explicitly organized as the means whereby pupils may attain the desired objectives, whatever these may be. In keeping with the earlier argument, the planning of a curriculum, or any part of it, is here seen as a logical nonsense until the objectives being aimed at are made clear. At this level general statements of aims have to be translated into statements of specific objectives to which curriculum activities can be explicitly directed. Such specification is far from easy and, as yet, no universal categories in which to carry it out are agreed upon. The celebrated *Taxonomy of Educational Objectives* by B. S. Bloom and his colleagues,[2] two volumes of which have so far appeared, is an important first attempt at a comprehensive scheme. It divides the whole area into cognitive, affective, and psychomotor domains, endeavoring to list classes of detailed objectives that might be pursued in each. In the cognitive domain, for instance, the categorization lists knowledge of specific items of information, of terminologies, conventions, classifications, and generalizations. Different types of intellectual abilities and skills are distinguished. In the affective domain there are, for instance, classes of different types of dispositions to respond, ranging from mere acquiescence to enjoyment, and classes of types of valuing. But valuable though this attempt may be in certain respects, it shows no awareness of the fundamental, necessary relationships between the various kinds of objectives that can be distinguished. A knowledge of the meaning of terms can certainly be thought of as in a different category from a knowledge of empirical facts or an acceptance of a rule of behavior. But clearly, in any given case, an achievement in one of these categories might be interrelated, even necessarily, with achievements in the others. Much knowledge of facts about, say, the weather, presupposes a knowledge of the meaning of appropriate terms, and accepting certain rules of behaviour might be justifiable only on a basis of such facts. Thus when it comes to deciding the curriculum objectives which we wish to pursue, we cannot behave as though they are independent elements that can even be characterized, let alone achieved, in isolation from each other. And to say this is but to put in another form what has been argued in Chapter 3 about the nature of those desirable states of mind with which education in its specific sense is centrally concerned, that fundamental to all these are those distinct, public modes of experience and knowledge which man has now achieved. What we need for satisfactory curriculum planning, then, is a grasp of the structure or pattern of relationships there is between the objectives in which we are interested. Mapping objectives in this way is an immensely complex philosophical task demanding much detailed analytical work in epistemology and the philosophy of mind. Little of this has as yet been done. Yet from the work there is, one or two tentative general conclusions can be drawn about this structure that are clearly of great importance for curriculum decisions.

It has been argued that, underlying all the more sophisticated objectives such as autonomy, creativeness, and critical thought, there must necessarily be the achievements of objective experience, knowledge, and understanding. If this is so, it suggests that the logically most fundamental objectives of all are those of a cognitive kind, on the basis of which, out of which, or in relation to which, all others must be developed. For only in so far as one has the relevant knowledge and forms of reasoning can a person be creative or critical in, say, atomic physics. Only in so far as one understands other people can one come to care about them and actively seek their good. Enjoying and valuing the arts is impossible without the concepts that make aesthetic experience available. The fundamental structure of the objectives would therefore seem to be within the domain of objective experience and knowledge. If we can map the relationships of achievements here, there is hope that we might eventually progress to a grasp of the more complex pattern of the elements built on these. What, then, are the basic achievements that are necessary to objective experience and knowledge, and what structure does there seem to be within this domain?

(b) *Modes of knowledge and experience.* Let us begin by noting that there can be no experience or knowledge without the acquisition of the relevant concepts. Further, it is only when experience and thought, which necessarily involve the use of concepts of some sort, involve those shared in a public world that the achievements with which we are concerned are possible. Without shared concepts there can be no such distinctions as those between fact and fantasy, truth and error. Only where there is public agreement about the classification and categorization of experience and thought can we hope for any objectivity within them. But merely shared concepts are insufficient for what we mean by objectivity. Connected with these concepts must be objective tests for what it is claimed is experienced, known or understood. Such tests are perhaps best exemplified by the tests of observation in the sciences, though there would seem to be no good reason for considering science to be the only objective pursuit. The crucial point is that, though objective judgments are not possible without a body of agreed concepts, the judgments themselves are not matters of further agreement. It is only because we agree on the meanings of the words employed that we can understand the claim that over five million people live in the Greater London area. Whether or not that claim is true is, however, not a matter of further agreement, but of objective test. Any agreement there may be amongst us about this claim is not just a matter of our deciding but is properly thrust on us by what is the case. And that remains true whether we are concerned with what is the case about the world, God, a work of art, or a moral action. It is, therefore, only through the mastery of a body of public concepts, with their related objective tests, that objective experience and knowledge can be achieved. And, if this is so, then the basic structure of objectives we are after must be one within that body of concepts and related tests which man has so far developed.

In looking for this structure it is not appropriate here to discuss the detail of relations between the particular concepts which we might wish to teach, for we are concerned only with the more general features of these relations that are significant for overall curriculum planning. What we really want to know at this general level is whether the domain of objective experience and knowledge is, for example, one complex body of interrelated concepts, a unity of some sort, a number of similar forms of experience and knowledge with parallel relations between the concepts in each area, or whether it has some other implicit organization. To answer this question necessitates an examination of the conceptual relations embedded in the many forms of public expression we have and of the serious claims to objective tests that are associated with these. An examination of this scope cannot be undertaken here; for this we must refer the reader elsewhere. Much of the work in this area is controversial, yet it seems to us to indicate a differentiation of modes of experience and knowledge that are fundamentally different in character.

Detailed studies suggest that some seven areas can be distinguished, each of which necessarily involves the use of concepts of a particular kind and a distinctive type of test for its objective claims. The truths of formal logic and mathematics involve concepts that pick out relations of a general abstract kind, where deducibility within an axiom system is the particular test for truth. The physical sciences, on the other hand, are concerned with truths that, in the last analysis, stand or fall by the tests of observation by the senses. Abstract though the theoretical concepts they employ may be, the sciences necessarily employ concepts for what is seen, heard, felt, touched or smelled, for it is with an understanding and knowledge of the sensible world that they are concerned. To be clearly distinguished from knowledge and experience of the physical world is our awareness and understanding of our own and other people's minds. Concepts like those of "believing," "deciding," "intending," "wanting," "acting," "hoping," and "enjoying," which are essential to interpersonal experience and knowledge, do not pick out, in any straightforward way, what is observable by the senses. Indeed the phrase "knowledge without observation" has been coined to make this point. The precise nature of the grounds of our objective judgments in this area is not yet adequately understood, though their irreducibility to other types of test can perhaps be most readily seen in judgments of our own states of mind. Moral judgment and awareness necessitate, in their turn, another family of concepts such as "ought," "wrong," and "duty." Unless actions or states are understood in such terms, it is not their moral character of which we are aware. The claim to objectivity in the case of moral judgments is a matter of long-standing dispute, but the sustained attempts there have been to show the objectivity of morals, and its irreducibility to other forms of knowledge, make this domain one which must be recognized as having serious claims to independent status. Likewise the claims for a distinctive mode of objective aesthetic experience, using forms of symbolic expression not confined to the linguistic, must be taken seriously, even though much philosophical work remains to be done here. Religious claims in their traditional forms certainly make use of concepts which, it is now maintained, are irreducible in character. Whether or not there are objective grounds for what is asserted is again a matter on which much more has yet to be said. The case would certainly seem to be one that cannot be simply dismissed. Finally philosophical understanding, as indicated in Chapter 1, would seem to involve unique second-order concepts and forms of objective tests irreducible to those of any first-order kind.

The differentiation of these seven areas is based on the claim that, in the last analysis, all our concepts seem to belong to one of a number of distinct, if related, categories which philosophical analysis is concerned to clarify. These categories are marked out in each case by certain fundamental, ultimate, or categorial concepts of a most general kind which other concepts in the category presuppose. It will be remembered that the difference between the "form" and "content" of experience was held, in Chapter 3, to be of crucial importance in giving an account of the development of modes of experience. It is these categorial concepts that provide the form of experience in the different modes. Our understanding of the physical world, for instance, involves such categorial concepts as those of "space," "time," and "cause." Concepts such as those of "acid," "electron," and "velocity," all presuppose these categorial notions. In the religious domain, the concept of "God" or "the transcendent" is presumably categorial whereas the concept of "prayer" operates at a lower level. In the moral area the term "ought" labels a concept of categorial status, as the term "intention" would seem to do in our understanding of persons. The distinctive type of objective test that is necessary to each domain is clearly linked with the meaning of these categorial terms, though the specific forms the tests take may depend on the lower-level concepts employed. This can be seen especially in the different sciences, different tests all presupposing the same categorial notions.

The division of modes of experience and knowledge suggested here is thus a fundamental categorial division, based on the range of such irreducible categories which we at present seem to have. That other domains might, in due course, come to be distinguished, is in no sense being prejudged, for the history of human consciousness would seem to be one of progressive differentiation. The categorization that is at present being suggested may in fact be inaccurate in detail. Be that as it may. What we are suggesting is that within the domain of objective experience and knowledge, there are such radical differences of kind that experience and knowledge of one form is neither equatable with, nor reducible to, that of any other form. In each case it is only by a grasp of the appropriate concepts and tests that experience and knowledge of that kind become available to the individual. Achievements in one domain must be recognized as radically different from those in any other. What is more, within any one domain the concepts used, and the objective claims made, form a particular network of relations. In some cases concepts are tightly connected in a pattern of necessary dependence. In others the relations are more complex and difficult to specify. The forms of justification likewise differ. Thus the concepts and claims of the domain can only be grasped in their varied relations to each other.

But the radical independence which each of these modes has in relation to the others, is only one aspect of the situation. What is also important is the pattern of interrelationships between them. On a moment's reflection it can immediately be seen that, however independent the domain of science may be, our understanding of the physical world is tightly dependent on our mathematical knowledge. It is also a commonplace that scientific discoveries involve us in new moral dilemmas. Equally some religious claims presuppose historical truths, whilst others demand moral understanding. Yet these interrelations must not be thought to weaken in any way the claims for independence made above. That experience or knowledge in one domain is *necessary* to that of another in no way implies that it is *sufficient*. Of itself no amount of mathematical knowledge is sufficient for solving a scientific problem; nor is science alone able to provide moral understanding. What we must recognize is that the development of knowledge and experience in one domain may be impossible without the use of elements of understanding and awareness from some other. But even when incorporated into another domain these elements retain their own unique character and validity. The observable features of an event remain such, no matter what religious interpretation may be offered of it. That an appeal to certain empirical facts may be necessary to justifying a moral principle means that there is a scientific prerequisite for moral understanding in this case. But that prerequisite must be judged by appropriate scientific canons, and its establishment is independent of the moral principle under consideration. And, granted the scientific truth, its significance for the moral principle can be judged only by moral canons. At this point the scientific canons now become irrelevant. It thus seems that the form of interrelationship between the independent domains of knowledge and experience can only be properly understood by recognizing first the basic differences between them, and then by seeing how they are interlocked when one domain employs elements of another without any loss to the independent character of each.

(c) *The selection of objectives.* The fundamental structural relations, which have been briefly sketched, have numerous implications for the choice of educational objectives to be served by a curriculum. Foremost among these is the fact that, if education is understood as developing desirable states of mind characterized by knowledge and understanding, we must decide with which of the several fundamentally different types of knowledge and understanding we are concerned. To educate a person significantly in some of these only is to limit the forms of his development which we are prepared systematically to pursue. The issue of breadth in education as opposed to narrow specialization is, if faced properly, surely the issue of whether or not a person is being significantly introduced to each of the fundamentally different types of objective experience and knowledge that are open to men. Not to try to introduce pupils to certain areas, or to give up too soon when the going becomes hard, is to accept that in these areas the individual will, as far as the school is concerned, develop no further. Admittedly what can be achieved in any area is a matter of degree. Yet experience would suggest that, only after sustained attention to the relevant concepts, the patterns of reasoning and tests for judgment peculiar to any domain, do these elements of thought function spontaneously in a clear and coherent way. It is therefore not surprising that there is a persistent call that general education shall be maintained for all throughout the secondary school stage.

The adequate development of general education has not only suffered from a lack of clarity about the range of understanding and knowledge it should pursue. It has also suffered from a failure to distinguish between the precise objectives of general education and those of special education within the same domain of knowledge and experience. A budding specialist needs a detailed knowledge of all the relevant concepts, skills, and tests for truth that will progressively provide him with a comprehensive understanding within a given domain. In this area his knowledge and experience will eventually stretch far beyond the confines of everyday contexts. A general education, however, aims at no such exhaustive mastery. Its concern is that the pupil will be sufficiently immersed in each form of understanding to appreciate its character, to employ its major elements that have application within the context of everyday life, and to be aware of the further possibilities in each area, given the time and inclination to pursue these. Clearly there can be an endless variety of courses in any area, the concern of which is a blend of these two. What we need, however, is undoubtedly the working out of the detailed objectives for courses, say, in English literature, which are appropriate, on the one hand, for the sixteen-year-old school leaver of average ability, and, on the other, for the sixteen-year-old "O" Level candidate who may or may not be going to specialize further in this domain. Equally we need them for the eighteen-year-old entrant to engineering studies at a polytechnic and for the eighteen-year-old university entrance scholar in English literature.

We have been at pains to emphasize, on philosophical grounds, the significance for the pupil's development of choosing certain educational objectives rather than others. By our choice of objectives we are deciding how far his scientific, aesthetic, or religious development is or is not important. In making the choice, however, it must not be forgotten, as was mentioned at the outset, that there are legitimate social demands for specific objectives that intelligent planning cannot ignore. A degree of specialized knowledge and skill in some limited area may be a necessity for all of us, for the good of the whole community as much as for our own individual good. At the present time the balance of forms of specialist training needed in our own society is as yet little more than a matter of speculation. Our choice must also take into account the relevant psychological knowledge we have of human abilities and motivation to learn. Just how far we are, at will, able to determine the pattern of development of any one individual, given our present methods of teaching and upbringing, is a controversial question. Certainly at present not everyone could be turned into a Newton or an Einstein, try as best we might. A rationally defensible curriculum must be planned to reach objectives that are defensible and that not only from a philosophical point of view.

Philosophy can seek to outline the nature and interrelation of objectives, thus indicating what coherent selection necessitates. It can indicate, too, the significance in human development of certain choices. It cannot go further alone.

Curriculum Organization

(a) *The means-ends model.* Once granted a set of desired objectives, diverse in their character and complex in their interrelations, the business of curriculum planning becomes the organization of the best means to achieve these ends. Yet expressed in this way the situation is liable to be misunderstood. For though the means-ends model brings out well that, logically, the objectives must be determined before all else, it is often taken to imply that no particular means are logically necessary for reaching the stated ends, and that the ends and the means can be characterized in complete independence of each other. A fountain pen may be the means whereby a certain shape is drawn on a piece of paper, but clearly quite other means could be used, and the shape outlined has no significant connection of a logical sort with the nature of the fountain pen used. But in the case of the curriculum, looked at from one point of view, the means employed may be, and often are, closely interrelated with the ends. Only if one understands how to solve certain types of algebraic equations can problems about planetary motion be solved by Newtonian mechanics. Learning the algebraic techniques can therefore harmlessly be regarded as a means to an understanding of planetary motion. But it is not one of many alternative means here, the best of which could be decided by empirical investigation. A grasp of Newtonian mechanics logically necessitates an understanding of these equations. The means and the end are here inseparably connected so that the latter is not even characterizable without appeal to the former. Indeed, in many cases the means to certain ultimate objectives can be broken down into the achieving of a series of subordinate but necessary objectives, which may be both valuable objectives in themselves and even logically necessary to the achievement of the ultimate objectives. Up to a point the interrelations between objectives can necessitate a certain sequence within the curriculum.

Looked at from another point of view, the means to the curricu-

lum's objectives consists of a program of activities specifically selected and organized to bring about the forms of development that
are desired. The distinctive character of these educational activities
will be discussed in the next chapter. But of interest at this juncture,
because of its close connection with the structure of objectives we
have outlined, is the type of units which curriculum organization
may involve.

(b) *The nature of school "subjects."* Clearly any realistic attempt
to achieve objectives of the variety and complexity pursued in modern education must somehow break the enterprise down into a number of limited tasks of manageable proportions. Traditionally this has
been done by organizing the curriculum into so-called school "subjects" such as arithmetic, history, English, religious education, and
woodworking. Under each of these headings a limited range of objectives is pursued to the exclusion of all others, and activities particularly appropriate for these ends are planned within each unit. Regular
periods of time are usually allotted to these activities according to
the importance attached to the objectives in each case. But on what
principle are these units constructed? Is there any reason to think
that this is the only, or even the best way of organizing learning? It is
tempting to try to defend this organization on the ground that it,
and it alone, is based on the radical differences which we have been
concerned to bring out between distinct independent modes of objective experience and knowledge. On examining a typical list of
subjects, however, it is obvious that they do not by any means all
pursue a group of objectives within one such mode. Under English,
or geography, or religious education, several types of understanding
may be sought at once. And this simple fact brings to the fore the
important point that curriculum units, whatever their character may
be—subject, topic, project or some other—must be seen as units constructed simply for educational purposes. They have no ultimate
value outside this context. Because our experience and knowledge is
differentiated into a number of distinct forms, it does not at all
follow that the best way of developing such knowledge and experience is to organize a curriculum in terms of these forms. There may
be many psychological factors about learning and motivation which
would argue against such a pattern. Social demands on the curriculum may make it desirable to bring together knowledge and understanding from different modes. On philosophical grounds alone, any

curriculum composed of subjects, each structured to objectives within one mode, would do scant justice to the complex interrelations between the modes that have already been pointed out. Developing a person's knowledge and experience necessarily involves developing these in the different modes, but that does not mean that one must concern oneself with each of these separately in isolation from all others. All understanding of moral problems does not have to be pursued in a context devoid of any concern for aesthetic appreciation, just because the two modes are of radically different kinds. The two can indeed both be developed, at least in part, by the use of certain works of English literature.

The process of developing different forms of distinct yet interrelated experience and understanding can be likened to building a jigsaw. One procedure with a jigsaw puzzle might be to structure the enterprise by attending in turn to patches of different colors; so one might attend to particular independent modes of experience within a curriculum. But there is no necessity to do so. One might equally compose the puzzle by attending to the outlines of different objects and characters drawn on the surface, no matter what colors are involved. One might instead, at least in the early stages, begin by placing the pieces that form the outer edges. In fact there are many different systematic procedures for building a jigsaw puzzle, all of which, however, result in the same interlocked and structured achievement. The same is true with the curriculum. Quite different types of curriculum unit may be used but, if they are effective, they will all necessarily result in the progressive achievement of the structured set of objectives that are desired. In any effective procedure, just as the colored patches must necessarily be composed in the puzzle, so the independent modes of understanding and experience must be built from the necessary interlocking elements in the curriculum. It therefore seems that, though the objectives, in which we are interested, must be seen to be related to each other in a structure of independent modes of experience and knowledge, it is possible to pursue these ends within a variety of curriculum units. Certain units might be devoted to objectives within a single mode, as, for instance, in the study of arithmetic. Others, as in the case of a subject like geography, or in a project, say on local industry, may be concerned with objectives taken from several different modes.

Yet if what matters is that the desired objectives be reached in their interrelated structure, though there may be no one universal way of achieving these, it would seem likely that there are some restrictions on the design of effective curriculum units which will spring from the nature of the structure which is to be built. It is, after all, perfectly possible to think of systematic ways of approaching a jigsaw puzzle which would in fact never succeed in fitting it together. One might, for instance, try to place all the pieces having an area of one square inch first, then move on to those with an area of 1.2 square inches, and so on. In curriculum planning one might try to produce units by grouping together objectives in ways that pay no attention to the other objectives with which they are necessarily interrelated. The strength of units devoted to a single mode of experience and knowledge is that they permit systematic attention to be given to the progressive mastery of closely interrelated concepts, patterns of reasoning, and qualities of mind, by radically restricting the character of the objectives with which they are concerned. Although elements from other modes may be used within such "subjects," the mastery of these is assumed to have been dealt with elsewhere. Such units, of course, stress the independence of the different modes.

(c) *Curriculum integration.* The more well-established subjects which are concerned with objectives of more than one mode, as, say, geography or English, have unusually been relatively restricted in the range of modes involved. In recent years, however, there has been pressure for them to extend their interests ever wider. Under the label of English, for instance, it is now not uncommon to find concern for an understanding of other persons and of moral matters, as much as aesthetic and linguistic elements. Such subjects have become important in emphasizing the connections which exist between different independent domains. The problem with them has always been that of developing adequately a mastery of elements within the several quite different types of experience and knowledge concerned, without sustained and systematic attention to these individually. Not surprisingly, when effectively pursued, they have repeatedly broken down into the distinct study of different aspects belonging to the various modes involved. This problem becomes acute, if not insuperable, with the topic or project type of curriculum unit where objectives from many modes are brought together. Where the objectives can be effectively reached by these means, and where the interrelation between those which the topic or project pursues is genuine and not artificial, such units have an important function.

Yet, to be successful, such work necessarily makes vast demands on the knowledge and ability of the teachers involved. In less competent hands, project and topic work can only too easily degenerate into pursuits which, however interesting, have little or no educational value. If the objectives from the different domains are not being adequately related to the structures within each of these, little is likely to be achieved. If the objectives grouped together have no significant relationship to each other, there seems little point to this exercise, which serves only to draw attention away from the necessary interrelations which objectives necessarily have within the separate modes. One wonders what is gained by organizing a project on hands concerned with physiology, the conditions of employment of factory hands, and the religious significance of the laying on of hands. Above all, there would seem to be an ever-present danger that this form of curriculum organization be allowed to determine what educational objectives it shall serve. A topic or project that provides an excellent way into learning elements within one of the modes is of no wider educational value if the only elements of other modes with which it is significantly related are either known already, or are of little educational importance, or are inappropriate for pupils at this stage. There would seem to be something seriously wrong with any form of education in which the organization of the means becomes more important than the ends it serves.

Yet, if a doctrinaire insistence on integrated curriculum units may be seriously miseducative, such units nevertheless would seem to have a crucial place in really adequate curriculum planning. The traditional subject curriculum has, both in complex subjects like geography and general science and in attempts at keeping in step interrelated subjects like mathematics and physics, at times gone some way to prevent an artificial isolation of certain domains. What it has not been able to do so successfully, however, is adequately to plan for those educational objectives which of their logical nature demand an integrated approach. This is most conspicuously the case if we think of the demands of adequate education in the making of practical, and especially moral, judgments. Judgments as to what ought to be done in personal and social affairs can only be validly made on the basis of a great deal of knowledge—of the physical world, of society, of the interests and feelings of other people, of the principles on which objective moral judgment must rest. Even efficiency judgments in everyday life, as well as in technical situations, can demand attention to many different factors. Adequate education in this area thus needs, at the very least, to develop the ability to recognize the relevance of very diverse considerations in these cases, and the ability to bring them together in a responsible practical judgment. These are clearly not easy to develop, but what is of importance in this context is that such education necessarily demands an integration of knowledge and understanding from many of the different domains. This being so, it is hard to see how the use of topics and projects can possibly here be avoided. If, in addition to the making of judgments, the related practical arts and skills for carrying out the decisions are also accepted as objectives, the argument for having both topics and projects in the curriculum would seem to be conclusive.

The issue of whether or not a curriculum should be composed solely of independent subjects or of other, integrated units, is thus not simply one of the most effective and efficient means of teaching and learning in areas where both approaches are possible. Clearly integrated units, simply by virtue of their complexity, can be the means of much valuable learning of many different kinds and from a motivational point of view may have much to recommend them. Yet behind this level of discussion lie considerations of the nature of the objectives being aimed at. Just as it is hard to see how the distinctive character of logically distinct modes of knowledge and experience can possibly be understood without some separate systematic attention to them, so it is hard to see how, without the use of properly designed integrative units, the complex interrelations of the domains can be adequately appreciated. The unfortunate polarization of curriculum debate into an opposition between the "traditional" devotees of subjects and the "progressive" devotees of integration, can here, as elsewhere, be seen to rest, at least in part, on philosophical misunderstandings on both sides. The nature of educational objectives demands that adequate attention be paid to developing systematically the pupil's grasp of modes of experience and knowledge which are both independent and yet intimately interrelated. To fail to attend to either of these aspects by sheer oversight, or in the name of some ill-considered theory of the unity of knowledge, is to distort the whole enterprise.

In discussing the organization of the curriculum we have confined ourselves to the nature of the units formed by grouping objectives. Such units would seem to be a practical necessity in all curriculum planning. Just how such units might be employed has not, however, been considered. Traditionally 40-45-minute periods have been allotted to different subjects. Yet clearly it is sometimes possible to do away with such an arrangement, leaving the detailed allocation of time to individual teachers or to individual pupils. The curriculum units employed in an "integrated day" may in fact be as subject structured as those in the most traditional grammar school curriculum. Changes in curricula are not always quite what they seem at first sight. This is equally true in another respect; for calls for the integration of the curriculum are not infrequently confused with calls for the introduction of new types of learning and teaching activity. Indeed it is important to recognize that, at times, we are asked to accept a quite unnecessary package deal, which links an organization of curriculum units with the introduction of new teaching methods. But whether the units of a curriculum are subjects based on independent modes of experience and knowledge, or subjects concerned with several such modes, or topics of some kind, or combinations of all these, it is equally possible to use the widest variety of modern methods. Team teaching, individual and group discussion work, the use of teaching machines, films, visits, and chalk and talk, these and all others can be used equally with a subject-structured curriculum as with any other. In rational curriculum planning questions about the structure of the curriculum must be kept clearly distinct from questions about the best activities and methods to be used. About the latter we have so far said practically nothing. To the distinctive character of educational activities we must now turn our attention.

Notes

1. In this essay references to chapters 1, 2, and 3 are to earlier chapters in *The Logic of Education,* the titles of which are: "Philosophy," "Education," and "Development," respectively.

2. Benjamin S. Bloom (ed.), *Taxonomy of Educational Objectives: The Classification of Educational Goals, Handbook 1: Cognitive Domain* (New York: Longmans, Green & Co., 1956); David R. Krathwohl, Benjamin S. Bloom, and Bertram B. Masia, *Taxonomy of Educational Objectives, Handbook II: Affective Domain* (New York: David McKay Company, Inc., 1964).

Selected References for Academic Rationalism and the Structure of Knowledge

Bestor, Arthur. *The Restoration of Learning* (New York: Knopf, 1955).

Ford, G. W., and L. Pugno (eds.). *The Structure of Knowledge and the Curriculum* [with articles by Schwab, Scriven, Lange, Wilson] (Chicago: Rand-McNally, 1964).

Hutchins, Robert M. *The Conflict in Education in a Democratic Society* (New York: Harper & Bros., 1953).

Koerner, James D. *The Case for Basic Education* (Boston: Little, Brown, 1959).

Thomas, John I. "Structure of—or for—Knowledge?" *Elementary School Journal* 72 (November 1971), 81-87.

Conclusion

Applying the Five Curricular Orientations to Man: A Course of Study

Elliot W. Eisner

Each contribution to this work was selected because it exemplified a particular orientation to curriculum planning. In the opening chapter we identified these orientations as the development of cognitive processes, curriculum as technology, as consummatory experience, for social reconstruction and relevance, and as academic rationalism. It is our view that most of the proposals for curriculum reform and most of the curricula that have been developed for use in the schools reflect one or more of these orientations in different degrees. That is, writers on curriculum and makers of curriculum employ beliefs or values that are characterized by one or more of these five orientations. The selections, all of which are in some way about curriculum, stand as examples of each of the orientations.

But what of curriculum itself? To what extent do the programs that have been built for use in the schools reflect or derive from the ideas found within the five curriculum orientations? Can the categories we have delineated be used as a screen for analyzing curricula? In this brief chapter we will examine one important and widely used curriculum—*Man: A Course of Study*—and analyze its form, content, and assumptions, using the five orientations to curriculum that we have formulated as analytical tools. We shall first describe some of the important features of *Man: A Course of Study*.[1]

Man: A Course of Study is a social studies curriculum designed for students in the middle and upper grades of the elementary school. The course, in its own words, "consists of books, films, posters, records, games and other classroom material. More importantly, it consists of a set of assumptions about man." The nature of these assumptions about man is reflected in the major questions it asks: What is human about man? How did he get that way? What can make him more so?

The course consists of over sixty lessons, each one a topic of study with its own aim. These topics might require one or more class periods and include such subjects as salmon, herring gulls, natural selection, baboons, the Netselik world, the hunting way of life, Netselik families, the dangers of winter, the hunting way of life in winter, winter camp, and the long gaze. For each topic a particular period of instructional time is suggested, although teachers are urged to use as much time as they feel appropriate for the particular children with whom they are working.

The materials include a series of booklets written for teachers. These booklets interpret the overall aims of the curriculum, set its tone, and explicate the content the children will be studying. In addition, the books provide annotated bibliographies and suggest a variety of activities that teachers might help children initiate in the classroom. Indeed, as much or more material is provided for the edification of the teacher as the student.

With this brief description of *Man: A Course of Study,* we turn now to an analysis of this curriculum proposal in terms of each of the orientations presented in this book. The analysis will seek to reveal those features of the curriculum that fit the values embedded in the orientations.

If we were to locate or build a curriculum mainly concerned with the development of cognitive processes, we would expect that it would identify, at least for teachers, the particular processes it was attempting to foster. The curriculum would be expected also to identify either a hierarchy of different processes (as is done in B. S. Bloom's taxonomy with its six hierarchical levels)[2] or to describe a sophisticated use of a particular process. In addition, a curriculum that concerned itself primarily with the development of cognitive processes would probably emphasize a dialectic, or problem-solving, or discovery approach to teaching; it would shun didacticism by attempting to get students involved in the process of inquiring so that their intellectual skills would be sharpened.

Man: A Course of Study does not present to either teacher or student a classification of the specific cognitive processes it seeks to foster. Instead, it presents topics and questions that are designed to foster engagement with the material, hoping that this process will enable children to enjoy the use of their minds. The material presented within the various topics is loosely sequenced, and the teacher is told at the outset that "a lesson plan is not a script." Clearly, the writers of the material envision the teacher in a central role, not simply as a conduit for someone else's material.

As one reads the material it becomes clear that heuristic questions —questions that stimulate curiosity and generate speculation and open-ended answers—are used generously. Teachers are given examples of such questions at the end of each topic. From such material the impression develops that, although the curriculum developers did not see fit to develop learning activities around a structured system of cognitive operations (as, for example, *Science: A Process Approach* does),[3] they were interested in stimulating curiosity and in encouraging analytic and speculative activities on the part of the students. What makes *Man: A Course of Study* less a cognitive process orientation than some other nationally developed curricula is what it chooses to emphasize. It is heavily committed to enabling children to understand ideas that its authors consider important. These ideas happen to be about man and the way in which he differs from other animals. The intellectual models it employs to get such ideas across to students are disciplinary in character. For example, children are shown examples of field notes and are informed about what ethnologists and anthropologists do to construct ideas about animals and men. The intended intellectual yield is more in the nature of important empirical generalizations about man, animals, and life styles than in refining the students ability to analyze or synthesize information.

This observation is not intended to assert that no analytic or synthetic processes come into play in dealing with the material in this curriculum. It is simply a way of saying that the development of cognitive processes per se does not appear to be the primary goal.

Man: A Course of Study can also be viewed from a technological orientation. Those who take a technological orientation to curricu-

lum almost always require that objectives be stated in specific, un-
ambiguous terms. If management of the curriculum by objectives is
to occur, which educational technologists considered desirable,
global, vague, or general statements of aims are not seen as useful.
Indeed, for some whose orientation to curriculum is technological,
objectives and test items to be employed at the end of the course are
synonomous. Furthermore, the technological orientation usually prescribes a highly structured sequence of tasks, each of which builds
upon what has gone before and prepares for what is to come. In
addition, criterion measures are specified where possible so that clear
indicators of achievement are available to enable teachers to locate
breakdowns in the system for purposes of recycling.

To what extent does *Man: A Course of Study* reflect such an
orientation? The answer to that question is short: Very little. In the
first place, *Man: A Course of Study* states no behavioral, instructional, or performance objectives. There is no specific or detailed statement about what students are expected to be able to do at the end of
the course that they were not able to do at the beginning. There are
no tests for use by the teacher to diagnose the students' entry behavior, and there are no achievement tests to determine if the program
has succeeded. Instead, the curriculum writers attempt to help the
teacher understand the topic and its ideas by the materials they
provide and by the annotated bibliography they include. They expect the teacher to modify the content, pacing, and resources in light
of the characteristics of the children in the class. The authors state:
"In the end, however, the teacher must use her own style and judgment in both instruction and evaluation. The lesson plans are only a
framework within which the most challenging work is still to be
accomplished." In short, the writers conceived of their work not as
providing a specific set of instructions to be followed as a blueprint
for success, but rather as a collection of *potentially* educational
material that at best can be adapted for classroom use by an artful
teacher. This message comes through not only in the lack of specific
objectives and evaluation instruments but in the general tone of the
materials themselves. The materials are informal in tone, at times
almost chatty, and never condescending.

What about *Man: A Course of Study* from a consummatory or
personal relevance orientation? To what extent do the materials reflect the concerns and values of those who argue for the importance

of personal engagement and private meaning in education? In this regard one can do little better than to equivocate for at least three reasons. First, the curriculum is intended for use in a class situation; it does not emanate from the particular interests of particular children and, in this sense, like all prescribed programs, the student does not have a hand in generating his own educational purposes. The curriculum stands as a content that adults believe children should learn. While this does not preclude meaningful and satisfying personal engagement, it does tend to homogenize educational goals for all students. In that sense it can contribute to the disregard of the student's own interests and purposes.

Second, the writers of *Man: A Course of Study* have taken pains to include material that will engage the child affectively as well as intellectually, striving to use material that can be related to the child's current life. In that sense the curriculum is more than propedeutic. Indeed, some of the material, such as that dealing with the Netselik, is so emotionally powerful that writers have questioned its appropriateness for elementary school children. Thus, on the one hand, *Man: A Course of Study,* like all other large-scale curriculum development projects, can serve to reinforce the general neglect of the student's own purposes within the context of the school. On the other hand, it, about as much as any curriculum for elementary school children, includes materials and modes of presentation that are designed to be personally engaging.

Third, *Man: A Course of Study* deals with a contingency that attends the use of any curriculum: the manner in which it is used in the classroom. Whether the content and aims of the curriculum are adapted in such a way to enable individual children to experience the curriculum in a consummatory fashion will depend on what individual teachers do with the material. In the consummatory or personal relevance orientation to curriculum the need for artistry in teaching is crucial, more crucial than in the other orientations. Viewed from a purely consummatory orientation, *Man: A Course of Study* falls short, but, when compared to other types of nationally developed curricula in the social studies for elementary school children, it shows up quite favorably with respect to the criteria implicit in this curriculum orientation.

Two other orientations to curriculum concern using educational programs as instruments for social reconstruction, and for transmitting products and methods that constitute the various intellectual disciplines. How does *Man: A Course of Study* look from the vantage point of social reconstructionism? While it is certainly true that the questions that underly *Man: A Course of Study* (What is human about man? How did he get that way? What can make him more so?) are of utmost importance in generating a conception, not only of man's nature but of the conditions that will enable him to realize his humanity, the general thrust of the curriculum is not toward the reconstruction of society. The topics that children study are not related to action programs designed in some way to improve social life in the community in which they live. The curriculum is intended to enable children to understand important ideas about life and environment, about adaptation, and about the relationship of environment to man's values. Furthermore, it is designed to peak curiosity by posing questions that invite children to speculate and hypothesize. Yet no attempt is made to link the resulting insights to social needs within the child's own environment. No effort is made to encourage children to take forms of social action on either a collective or an individual level that will heighten their sense of social responsibility. Children are encouraged to use some of the observation techniques they have read about in interviewing families in their neighborhood, but this is encouraged to foster an understanding of one type of social science rather than as a precursor to social action. The scientific mode, the man of thought, the joy of discovery—these are dominant values embedded in *Man: A Course of Study*.

Man: A Course of Study is not intended to do everything. Yet, the values that it reflects are not likely to be those which would have children become increasingly sensitive to their responsibilities for building a better community. Schools in the Soviet Union, for example, make a conscious effort to build group solidarity among the young and to get elementary-aged children into groups that undertake community-oriented service tasks. For those in our own country who believe that one of our greatest educational needs is to foster a similar sense of social concern and social action, *Man: A Course of Study,* by virtue of its topics, moves in the right direction, but falls far short of what is both desirable and possible.

Academic rationalism, among the several curriculum orientations, is the one with the longest history. This orientation emphasizes the schools' responsibility to enable the young to share the intellectual fruits of those who have gone before, including not only the concepts, generalizations, and methods of the academic disciplines but also those works of art that have withstood the test of time. For those who embrace this curriculum orientation, becoming educated means becoming initiated into the modes of thought these disciplines represent or becoming informed about the content of those disciplines.

Because *Man: A Course of Study* makes such great use of social science concepts and methods and because it is concerned with helping children understand the relationship of method to conclusion, its tone is strongly academic rationalistic. The flavor of its material is academic in spirit as well as in fact. The introduction of students to ethnological methods, the selection of salmon and baboons as topics for study, the subtle introduction of how ethnologists do studies of animal behavior provide in their totality an introduction to some branches of social science. Curriculum writers seem to be interested in enabling children to think about the living world like young enthnologists and thus to share something in common with those who do so professionally. In emphasizing this orientation, a particular set of educational values is being expressed. It seems appropriate that those who select curriculum for use in the schools, as well as those who embark on the creation of curriculum, be aware not only of the orientation they are accepting but also of those they are neglecting.

The five orientations to curriculum that we have identified make it possible to "profile" an existing curriculum and to consider the dominant thrust of the curriculum being planned. Virtually all curricula that have been produced will reflect different degrees of each of the orientations we have described. The descriptions we have provided in the opening chapter are presented in their "pure" form for purposes of clarity; they function as educational prototypes. In the real world such "pure" forms are seldom found.

Notes

1. Educational Development Center, Social Studies Curriculum Project, *Man: A Course of Study* (Cambridge, Massachusetts: Educational Development Center, 1968).

2. Benjamin S. Bloom (ed.), *Taxonomy of Educational Objectives: Handbook 1, Cognitive Domain* (New York: Longmans, Green & Co., 1956).

3. Commission on Science Education, American Association for the Advancement of Science, *Science: A Process Approach* (Washington, D. C.: the Association, 1963).